NOTES OF A NATIVE SON

Notes of a Native Son

JAMES BALDWIN

Beacon Press   *Boston*

Beacon Press
25 Beacon Street
Boston, Massachusetts 02108

Beacon Press books
are published under the auspices of
the Unitarian Universalist Association of Congregations.

97 96 95 94 93 92 91 90   8 7 6 5 4 3 2 1

ISBN 0-8070-0907-5
LCN 90-52598

FOR
PAULA MARIA
AND
GEBRIL

Contents

Acknowledgments

The author is grateful to the following publications for permission to reprint material that first appeared in their pages: *Commentary* for "Carmen Jones" (which appeared in the January 1955 issue as "Life Straight in De Eye"), "The Harlem Ghetto" (February 1948), and "Equal in Paris" (March 1955); *Harper's Magazine* for "Notes of a Native Son" (November 1955) and "Stranger in the Village" (October 1953); *The New Leader* for "Journey to Atlanta" (October 9, 1948); *Partisan Review* for "Everybody's Protest Novel" (June 1949), "Many Thousands Gone" (November-December 1951), and "A Question of Identity" (July-August 1954); and *The Reporter* for "Encounter on the Seine" (which appeared in the issue of June 6, 1950, as "The Negro in Paris").

Introduction
David A. Leeming

With the publication of *Notes of a Native Son* in 1955, James Baldwin staked a large claim in an area of American literary territory inhabited by such artists of the essay and autobiography as Ralph Waldo Emerson, Henry David Thoreau, and Frederick Douglass. Combining the powerful rhetoric of the Old Testament with a style that owes as much to Henry James as to the Bible, Baldwin speaks out in this collection with a voice at once passionately committed and devastatingly objective. The James Baldwin of 1955 was a writer who believed that "the only real concern of the artist" is "to recreate out of the disorder of life that order which is art." *Notes of a Native Son* is nothing if not a record of disorder redeemed by art.

The disorder that confronted the young James Baldwin was a force that continues to destroy the lives of the black dispossessed, and, as Baldwin so deftly argues, it is a disorder that has inevitably colored the psychic lives of those responsible for the dispossessing. "You're the nigger, baby," he once announced to an astonished Harvard audience, and that message is one of the essential elements of *Notes of a Native Son* as it is of Baldwin's writing in general.

In fact, although the idea for the collection was not the author's (it came from his school friend, the editor Sol Stein), *Notes of a Native Son* can bè said to constitute a James Baldwin manifesto, an overture to the story he was to tell for the rest of his life. Each of the major Baldwin themes is touched on here: the search for identity in a world that, because of its racial myths, cannot recognize reality; the acceptance of one's inheritance ("the conundrum of color is the inheritance of every American") as one claims one's birthright ("my birthright was vast, connecting me to all that lives, and to everyone, forever"); the loneliness of the artist's quest; the urgent necessity of love. The essays are the very first prophetic cries of a new version of the "bastard of the West," the "invisible man," the "stranger in the village," the man with "no name in the street" who cries, "Nobody knows my name."

Notes of a Native Son also set the autobiographical tone that was to characterize all of Baldwin's work — fiction and nonfiction alike. The special circumstances that confronted him from the day he realized he was black made the autobiographical approach inevitable: "I have not written about being a Negro at such length because I expect that to be my only subject, but only because it was the gate I had to unlock before I could hope to write about anything else" (p. 8). In the mid-1980s, as he wrote *Evidence of Things Not Seen*, he was still trying to unlock that gate, a fact indicative of both the beauty and the tragedy of Baldwin's life and work and of the moral failure of the society that held the key to the lock.

The essays contained in *Notes* were published between 1948 and 1955 in *Commentary, The New Leader, Partisan Review, The Reporter*, and *Harper's Magazine*, all leading "liberal" journals that, like Alfred A. Knopf, the publisher of Baldwin's first novel, *Go Tell It on the Mountain* in 1953, had recognized in Baldwin a voice that could penetrate old mental barriers, that could carry the message of African American deprivation into the living rooms of white America. The liberals were right. *Notes of a Native Son* was the "making" of James Baldwin for white America. It was also the source of a misconception that was to plague him throughout his career. "Why don't you write more essays like the ones in *Notes of a Native Son?*" he was constantly asked by whites. These readers appreciated and were subtly comforted by the fact that, in the *Notes* essays, when he is not speaking directly from a first-person autobiographical perspective, Baldwin tends to assume the point of view of "one of us" (white Americans) looking objectively and honestly at "them" (black Americans).

What it means to be a Negro is a great deal more than this essay can discover; what it means to be a Negro in America can perhaps be suggested by an examination of the myths we perpetuate about him. (p. 27)

We (Americans in general, that is) like to point to Negroes and to most of their activities with a kind of tolerant scorn; but it is ourselves we are watching, ourselves we are damning, or — condescendingly — bending to save. (p. 64)

Baldwin's method is to reach consciences by way of minds. He seduces the reader by presenting his message without resorting to the violence or the harshness of a work like Richard Wright's *Native Son* — a work from which he ironically took his own title. He holds our white hands as he leads us through the horrors of the black dilemma, not without passion, but with subtlety and literary polish.

White Americans are disturbed by the picture James Baldwin paints in *Notes*, but his point of view reassures us.

African American reaction was critical at times. In his review of *Notes* in *The New York Times Book Review* (28 February 1956), Langston Hughes suggested that "Baldwin's viewpoints are half American, half Afro-American, incompletely fused." Others have asked why the white man's hand should be held at all. Why, they ask, should harsh realities be presented in a placating manner? Baldwin's own prose, beginning with *The Fire Next Time*, increasingly suggests that he asked himself the same questions.

The problem of point of view in *Notes of a Native Son* must be confronted by anyone concerned with the question of appropriate audiences for "minority spokesmen." Baldwin's choice of point of view can best be understood through a consideration of the context in which the essays were written. These were the first essays of a writer who had escaped — from a repressive religion and an oppressive father, from the ghetto itself, and from the restrictions placed on him as a man and as a writer by the very existence of the ghetto and the reasons behind it. Rightly or wrongly, at this point in his career Baldwin felt that he must reveal his experience not in the form of protest literature, not as a "Negro writer," but as a writer pure and simple. In order to achieve this goal he had to reach out beyond the ghetto for his audience. The "liberal" journals were the logical place and the uninvolved objective point of view followed just as logically. "I want to be an honest man and a good writer," he wrote (p. 9), and this desire is what took him first to Greenwich Village and then to Paris. In both places he could continue his experience of an integrated way of life — first with bohemians and then with expatriates — that was rare in the first half of this century, an experience that had begun with his friendship with a young white school teacher in the early 1930s, and had developed through close friendships with schoolmates such as Richard Avedon, Sol Stein, and Emile Capouya at the De Witt Clinton High School in New York. In short, in the late 1940s and early 1950s Baldwin found it necessary to make a place for himself in the white world in order to broaden his base and his audience, thereby undermining the isolating power of the labels "colored," "Negro," and "Negro writer" that the world had pinned on him.

It was in part the fear of the label "Negro writer" that led him to make his celebrated "attacks" on Richard Wright in *Notes* and in *Nobody Knows My Name* (1961). But the departure from Harlem and the criticism of Wright as a protest writer did not mean that Baldwin had denied or broken away from his ethnic roots, his family, or friends like Beauford Delaney or even Wright himself — any more than he dropped his white friends in later years when he became more of a protest writer himself. Baldwin's approach to white America was never humble or self-denigrating; neither in *Notes* nor elsewhere was he ever in the least bit obsequious or apologetic. Baldwin often said that he left the pulpit to "preach the gospel." Whatever his technical point of view in *Notes*, he used those essays to bring to white America a prophetic message concerning the perilous state of a nation of blacks and whites — a nation he, the "native son," dared to call his own. Furthermore, even in the Greenwich Village and Paris years he never lost sight of his need to confront his "inheritance" as an American black in order to achieve his "birthright" as a man. In the

"Autobiographical Notes" in *Notes of a Native Son*, for example, he speaks admiringly of Ralph Ellison for being able to "utilize in language, and brilliantly, some of the ambiguity and irony of Negro life" (p. 8), and this achievement was always Baldwin's goal as well. The point is simply that at this stage in his career Baldwin needed the white world and a white audience if he was to establish himself as a writer and, ultimately, as a prophet. Prophets speak to the whole nation, and especially to those most in need of salvation. If, therefore, the passion of his writing can be traced to the language of the African American church he knew so well from his days as a child preacher in Harlem and from the blues of Bessie Smith, the cold objectivity, the relentless irony of his rhetoric came in great part from his understanding of the white culture he had to penetrate and help save if he was to achieve his birthright. It should come as no surprise that a second source for the title *Notes of a Native Son* was *Notes of a Son and Brother*, an autobiographical work by Henry James, another American whose expatriate status enabled him to observe his own nation more keenly.

Notes of a Native Son is divided into three parts. The first is concerned with the identity of the "Negro" and with the African American as artist. The second contains three essays on black life in America, culminating in the great autobiographical essay "Notes of a Native Son," which is the record of a painful search for self as well as for ethnic identity. The last part is made up of four essays written to America from the expatriate in Europe.

Part I begins with two *Partisan Review* essays originally written in 1949 and 1951 (the first was also published in the Parisian expatriate journal *Zero*, with which Baldwin had become closely involved). Both essays, "Everybody's Protest Novel" and "Many Thousands Gone," remain controversial to this day because they contain the famous criticism of Richard Wright. In a later essay called "Alas, Poor Richard" (1961) collected in *Nobody Knows My Name*, Baldwin recalls an encounter with Wright on the day the issue of *Zero* containing "Everybody's Protest Novel" appeared: "I walked into the Brasserie Lipp. Richard was there, and he called me over. . . .[He] accused me of having betrayed him, and not only him but all American Negroes by attacking the idea of protest literature" (p. 156).

"Everybody's Protest Novel" and "Many Thousands Gone" do indeed criticize the concept of protest literature, and Baldwin's treatment of Wright was perhaps insensitive, but Baldwin intended no betrayal of black America. His criticism of Wright is secondary to larger issues. Baldwin begins "Everybody's Protest Novel" by dismissing *Uncle Tom's Cabin*, which had been a favorite novel of his as a child. This "cornerstone of American social protest fiction" is a "very bad novel" which, because it is primarily a protest novel, ignores the real, "the carnal man, the man of the flesh." By extension, Richard Wright's failure is seen to be similar to Harriet Beecher Stowe's. Protest writers are concerned with theories and with the categorization of human beings, and however brilliant the theories or accurate the categorizations, "the failure of the protest novel lies in its rejection of life."

Although the two essays are of interest as critiques of protest literature and of Richard Wright, much more important is what they reveal about the development of the young James Baldwin's prophecy and his art. In criticizing Stowe and Wright, Baldwin is laying the foundation of his own position as a novelist and spokesperson. The real questions that lie behind the two essays are: What is an artist? What is a "Negro?" What is morality? As Baldwin sees it, the true artist must avoid the easy answers provided by theorization and categorization. The artist's job is to absorb and recreate not only the deeds of humanity but the motivations for those deeds, which spring from human ambiguity and complexity: "In overlooking, denying, evading [this] complexity — which is nothing more than the disquieting complexity of ourselves — we are diminished and we perish; only within this web of ambiguity, paradox, this hunger, danger, darkness, can we find at once ourselves and the power that will free us from ourselves" (p. 15). This is vintage Baldwin — the writer-prophet whose outcry against the theoretical rigidity of protest literature is the same as his denunciation of the theoretical blindness of prejudice and the same as his plea for the acceptance of humanity with all of its complexity, a plea that would soon take particularly moving form in *Giovanni's Room* (1956).

For Baldwin, the obligations of the artist are precisely those of the human being who would be morally free. The protest writer imprisons humanity. The co-opting of Wright's Bigger Thomas, that "monster created by the American republic," by socially earnest whites at the end of *Native Son*, reflects the all-too-prevalent assumption "that the black man, to become truly human and acceptable, must first become like us. . . . This assumption once accepted, the Negro in America can only acquiesce in the obliteration of his own personality" (p. 45). By the same token, in "Many Thousands Gone," Baldwin insists that what the white American feels about the black American is really a reflection of self-hatred and self-denial: "One may say that the Negro in America does not really exist except in the darkness of our minds. . . . Our dehumanization of the Negro then is indivisible from out dehumanization of ourselves" (pp. 24–25).

What Baldwin does in these essays, then, is to use Wright's fiction and protest literature in general as a background against which to establish his own approach to art and to life. Baldwin suggests that bad art and immorality have much in common. The artist choosing to deal in truth had better be concerned with articulating the manners, traditions, and rituals through which people have managed to survive in myths created by others. Certainly the artist who takes up the African American situation should bear this in mind along with such complicated questions as the literal and moral "blood relationship" between blacks and whites that is "perhaps the most profound reality of the American experience," a relationship that we cannot possibly understand "until we accept how very much it contains of the force and anger and terror of love" (p. 42). These are themes that took fictional form in works like *Another Country, Tell Me How Long the Train's Been Gone*, and *Just Above My Head*.

Part I is capped with a 1955 *Commentary* review of the all-black film, *Carmen Jones* (1955), a review originally published as "Life Straight in De Eye" and included here as "Carmen Jones: The Dark is Light Enough." Baldwin was to retain a life-long fascination with the cinema, which was fully expressed in the 1976 work *The Devil Finds Work*. In the *Carmen Jones* review, as in all of his comments on films, Baldwin is torn between an almost childlike love of the silver screen (the movies had been his only escape from the rigors of his early life) and the necessity of seeing in the films themselves — particularly American films — the reflection of social realities. As an all-black film, *Carmen Jones* had to be a thrilling experience for a young African American brought up on Lana Turner and Gary Cooper. But the astute social critic was quick to recognize that white Hollywood was using the beautiful "Negro bodies" in the film to perpetuate white myths of black sexuality. And once again the young Baldwin found an opportunity to articulate one of his major leitmotifs: "What is distressing is the conjecture this movie leaves one with as to what Americans take sex to be. . . . The most important thing about this movie . . . is that the questions it leaves in the mind relate less to Negroes than to the interior life of Americans" (p. 53). In short, "You're the nigger, baby." The idea that white myths about black sexuality reflect a perversion that inevitably follows from the dehumanizing of one race by another is an idea that would later be explored fictionally in such works as the *Blues for Mr. Charlie*, "Going to Meet the Man," and *Another Country*, to mention only a few examples.

The second part of *Notes of a Native Son* speaks directly to conditions in black America. The first essay, "The Harlem Ghetto," is one of Baldwin's first published works, written for *Commentary* early in 1948. As in the essays of part I, he takes the position here of a concerned but objective reporter, breaking the tone only rarely to reveal his own personal connection with his subject. The white reader is taken on a tour by a "native son" who has moved elsewhere and can look at his old "home town" with a chilling clarity. The journalist is ruthlessly honest: "Negro leaders have been created by the American scene, which thereafter works against them at every point" (p. 59). "It is the terrible dilemma of the Negro press that, having no other model, it models itself on the white press," the result being a parody of white society's moral bankruptcy: "Within the body of the Negro press all the wars and falsehoods, all the decay and dislocation and struggle of our society are seen in relief." Because the Negro press reflects the violence of a minority condemned by its very role model to violence, it becomes, "like the Negro, . . . the scapegoat for our ills" (p. 64). Religion in Harlem, thought to exemplify "the Negro's essential simplicity and good-will," is in fact "a fairly desperate and emotional business" concerned with white injustice and a longing for revenge (pp. 65–66). Baldwin ends this early preview of what will emerge later as *The Fire Next Time* (1963) with an extended comment on the relationship between Jews and black Americans. This was to remain a special concern of Baldwin. It surfaces, for example, in a *New York Times Magazine* article, "Negroes are Anti-Semitic Because They're Anti-White" (9 April 1967) and in controversial comments made in classes at the University of Massachusetts in the mid 1980s. In the "Harlem Ghetto" essay as in the later remarks on the subject he was brutally frank. Jews and blacks have a natural alliance based on racial oppression. Moreover, the African American church has traditionally expressed its longing for freedom in terms of Old Testament language referring to the captivity of the Jews and their search for the promised land. Yet the realities of racial discrimination — for Jews and blacks alike — mean that for the child growing up in Harlem the Jew is often the landlord or grocer demanding his payment. The Jew is the white person the black resident of Harlem is most likely to confront and, therefore, to hate, but not because he is a Jew:

The Negro, facing a Jew, hates, at bottom, not his Jewishness but the color of his skin. It is not the Jewish tradition by which he has been betrayed but the tradition of his native land. Just as a society must have a scapegoat, so hatred must have a symbol. Georgia has the Negro and Harlem has the Jew. (p. 72)

The second essay of part II, "Journey to Atlanta," was done for *The New Leader*, also in 1948. Ostensibly it is a recounting of the unpleasant experience of the Melodeers, a gospel quartet that included two of Baldwin's brothers and went to Atlanta to help the campaign of Henry Wallace's Progressive Party. In fact, the essay is a stunning attack on the Progressive Party and all other liberal groups that mask their racism in a dehumanizing commitment to political theory. The narrative, rich with the ruthless irony that later became a Baldwin trademark, is a foreshadowing of the ideas contained in "Everybody's Protest Novel" and "Many Thousands Gone." As long as the Melodeers behaved and performed as directed, they were treated as "representatives" of the black community. But as soon as their humanity surfaced and they wanted things like money, food, and shelter, they became "niggers" and were unceremoniously shipped home. "The Melodeers laugh about their trip now, that good-natured, hearty laughter which is, according to white men, the peculiar heritage of Negroes, Negroes who were born with the fortunate ability to laugh all their troubles away" (p. 84). The essay is an ironic metaphor for the situation of blacks in America. It is also the direct ancestor of the ironic masterpieces to come, works like *The Fire Next Time* and *No Name in the*

Street. Along with "The Harlem Ghetto" it serves as a preface to the title essay, "Notes of a Native Son," written in 1955 for *Harper's Magazine*, an essay that many have called Baldwin's best.

The writing of "Notes of a Native Son" was the second stage of a rite of passage for Baldwin, now a recognized author who had recently returned from Paris to the relative success of *Go Tell It on the Mountain*. The first stage had been the events that form the subject matter of "Notes." In *Go Tell It on the Mountain* Baldwin had reacted fictionally to his childhood in Harlem and particularly to his father (in fact, his stepfather), who remained an obsession with Baldwin until the day he died. In "Notes" he confronts the problem of his father directly, which is to say he faces the reasons for his father's bitterness and for the failure of their relationship by exploring his father's character and situation in the context of his own identity, and he does so with the same impeccable objectivity employed in the other essays of *Notes of a Native Son*. From the trouble he had had writing *Mountain* he knew that such an exploration would be necessary before he could write anything else. It is not surprising, then, that in "Notes" he creates a metaphorical role for himself, for his father, and for his house, a role that, as Horace Porter rightly suggests, owes something to the biblical story of the prodigal son (*Stealing the Fire* [Wesleyan University Press, 1989], pp. 23ff.). "Notes of a Native Son" is a parable of the return of the "native son" to his father's "house" — Harlem — and is a metaphor for the thirty-year-old James Baldwin's attempt to discover his father's legacy within himself and to rework that inheritance into something universal that will open the gate to his birthright as an artist and as a man. In this light, the coincidence of events in the autobiographical narrative becomes extraordinary. The death of David Baldwin, the father, himself a Pentecostal preacher, coincides with the Harlem riots of 1943, the return of the prodigal from his first escape to Greenwich Village, the prodigal's nineteenth birthday, and the birth of his "baby sister." The Harlem in ruins that the prodigal witnesses on the way to the graveyard becomes a metaphor for his own inner state as he gropes for his identity. It also symbolizes the plight of the nation whose prophet the prodigal will become by taking on — ironically, and in his own way — his father's mission as a preacher. "Notes of a Native Son" is the story of an epiphany, a calling, the achieving of a vocation.

In the first section of the three-part essay, Baldwin relives his father's bitterness and gradual descent into insanity and concludes that both can be traced to his repressive religious views, his denial of flesh-and-blood humanity (the sin of the protest novel), and ultimately to the horrors of racism. David Baldwin "knew that he was black but did not know that he was beautiful" (p. 87). The young Baldwin realizes that the "bitterness which had helped to kill my father could also kill me" (p. 88). He remembers his father's resentment, on racial grounds, of the young white teacher who had befriended him. And he recalls his own hatred of and attack upon a white waitress whose human individuality was buried in her role as a representative of the white world that refused to include him. As he looks back he realizes that his own life was endangered at that moment "not from anything other people might do but from the hatred I carried in my own heart" (p. 98).

In the second part of the essay Baldwin remembers his last visit with his father. There could be no reconciliation

because David Baldwin was unconscious and on the brink
of death. He was to die the next day, the same day on which
his daughter Paula was born. New life and hope seemed
to grow out of bitterness and death.

The final section contains memories of the funeral and
an attempt to learn from the message in his father's favorite
text: "Choose you this day whom you will serve . . . for
me and my house, we will serve the Lord." The revelation
comes to Baldwin on the drive to the graveyard, passing
the scenes of destruction left by the riots of the night before:
"bitterness was folly. It was necessary to hold on to things
that mattered" — the dead man, the new child, the future.
Out the memory of David Baldwin's bitter use of his text
came "an immutable law" that would serve the newly born
artist-prophet for a lifetime: "Hatred, which could destroy
so much, never failed to destroy the man who hated"
(p. 113). James Baldwin had begun to bury his father. In
later years he would learn even to love him.

The four essays that make up part III of *Notes of a Native
Son* grew directly out of Baldwin's life in Paris in the 1950s.
They are also records of an expatriate's attempt to discover
from a distance what it means to be an American. Like so
many themes in *Notes of a Native Son*, this one was to
continue to concern Baldwin throughout his career, particularly since he spent so many years living abroad.

"Encounter on the Seine: Black Meets Brown" first appeared in *The Reporter* in 1950 as "The Negro in Paris"
and concerns the frightening realization that the African
American has less in common with the African than with
white Americans. He is "bone of their bone, flesh of their
flesh; they have loved and hated and obsessed and feared
each other and his blood is in their soil. Therefore he cannot

deny them, nor can they ever be divorced" (p. 123). The inevitable need of the black American is "to establish himself in relation to [this] past" in order to achieve identity — once again, to challenge his inheritance in order to achieve his birthright. This need and this sense of alienation — which also affect white Americans, who are equally inheritors of the "conundrum of color" — cause Baldwin to conclude that a "depthless alienation from oneself and one's people is, in sum, the American experience" (p. 123).

The theme of identity is treated again in the 1954 *Partisan Review* essay called "A Question of Identity." This is perhaps the most Jamesian of Baldwin's essays. One feels at moments as if one were in the presence of a mid-twentieth-century Lambert Strether discussing the problems of Americans — in this case students — living abroad. The essay, in fact, is a revisiting of the problems James takes up in *The Ambassadors*, and was written at a time when Baldwin was particularly occupied with reading James. Lambert Strether might well have spoken of "the moment, so to speak, when one leaves the Paris of legend and finds oneself in the real and difficult Paris of the present" (p. 129), or of the "American confusion seeming to be based on the very nearly unconscious assumption that it is possible to consider the person apart from all the forces which have produced him" (p. 136). And surely Strether and James would have agreed that "from the vantage point of Europe [the American] discovers his own country" (p. 137).

But it is the style more than anything else that reminds us of James — the elegant and complex sentences that attempt to reveal so much at once, and always the irony:

What the European, in a thoroughly exasperating innocence, assumes is that the American cannot, of course, be divorced from the so diverse phenomena which make up his country, and that he is willing, and able, to clarify the American conundrum. If the American cannot do this, his despairing aspect seems to say, who, under heaven, can? (p. 129)

And

this so suddenly affirmative student is but changing the fashion of his innocence, nothing being more improbable than that he is now prepared, as he insists, to embrace his Responsibilities — the very word, in the face of his monumental aversion to experience, seems to shrink to the dimensions of a new, and rather sinister, frivolity. (p. 131)

The last two essays of *Notes of a Native Son* are so well known and so often anthologized that they require little introduction. "Equal in Paris" was published in *Commentary* in 1955 and "Stranger in the Village" in *Harper's Magazine* in 1953. Both are autobiographical narratives that suggest larger issues having to do with American identity. "Equal in Paris" is an ironical account of Baldwin's 1949 arrest in Paris. He was falsely accused by the police of having been an accomplice in the theft of a hotel sheet, and his case was dismissed, but only after he had spent several days, including Christmas, in jail. In the merriment in the court after the dismissal, James Baldwin the man becomes, as he so often does, James Baldwin the representative man, experiencing in the unfeeling "laughter of those who consider themselves to be at a safe remove from the wretched, for whom the pain of the living is not real," the universality of the arbitrary cruelty he had known so well in his native land (p. 158).

"Stranger in the Village" is perhaps Baldwin's most popular essay. It records his 1952 visit to the Swiss mountain village of his friend Lucien Happersberger, where he went, appropriately, to finish *Go Tell It on the Mountain*. Never having seen a black man, the villagers treat him in such a way as to make the village a model for Europe in an extended metaphor in which Baldwin is the alienated black race. The essay is an early example of Baldwin's assertion that America is different, that whatever white Americans might think, the deep and painful association with blacks has changed them forever: "No road whatever will lead Americans back to the simplicity of this European village where white men still have the luxury of looking on me as a stranger." And this is an "achievement," because it means, finally, that "this world is white no longer, and it will never be white again" (p. 175). No one who reads *Notes of a Native Son* can possibly doubt that conclusion.

Preface to the 1984 Edition
James Baldwin

It was Sol Stein, high school buddy, editor, novelist, playwright, who first suggested this book. My reaction was not enthusiastic: as I remember, I told him that I was too young to publish my memoirs.

I had never thought of these essays as a possible book. Once they were behind me, I don't, in fact, think that I thought of them at all. Sol's suggestion had the startling and unkind effect of causing me to realize that time had passed. It was as though he had dashed cold water in my face.

Sol persisted, however, and so did the dangers and rigors of my situation. I had returned from Paris, in 1954, out of motives not at all clear to me. I had promised a Swiss friend a visit to the land of my birth, but that, I think, has to be recognized as a pretext: it fails to have the weight of a motive. I find no objective reason for my return to America at that time — I am not sure that I can find the subjective one, either.

Yet, here I was, at the top of 1954, several months shy of thirty, scared to death, but happy to be with my family and my friends. It was my second return since my departure, in 1948.

I had returned in 1952, with my first novel, stayed long enough to show it to my family, and to sell it, and, then, I hauled on out of here. In 1954, I came back with *The Amen Corner*, and I was working on *Giovanni's Room* — which had broken off from what was to become *Another Country*.

Actually, '54–'55, in spite of frightening moments, and not only in retrospect, was a great year. I had, after all, survived something — the proof was that I was working. I was at the Writer's Colony, Yaddo, in Saratoga Springs, when my buddy, Marlon Brando, won the Oscar, and I watched Bette Davis present it to him, and kiss him, on TV. The late Owen Dodson called me there, from Washington, D.C., to say that he was directing, at Howard University, a student production of my play. I went to Washington, where I met the late, great E. Franklin Frazier and the great Sterling Brown. Howard was the first college campus I had ever seen, and, without these men, I do not know what would have become of my morale. The play, thank God, was a tremendous seven- or ten-day wonder, playing to standing room only on the last night, in spite of a reluctant, not yet Black faculty ("This play will set back the Speech Department by thirty years!"), a bewildered *Variety* ("What do you think Negroes in the North will think of this play?"), and the fact that it was not to be seen again for nearly ten years. And I had fallen in love. I was happy — the world had never before been so beautiful a place.

There was only one small hitch. I — we — didn't have a dime, no pot, nor no window.

Sol Stein returned to the attack. We had agreed on nine essays, he wanted a tenth, and I wrote the title essay between Owen's house and the Dunbar Hotel. Returned to New York, where I finished *Giovanni's Room*. Publisher's Row, that hotbed of perception, looked on the book with horror and loathing, refused to touch it, saying that I was a young *Negro* writer, who, if he published this book, would alienate his audience and ruin his career. They would not, in short, publish it, as a favor to me. I conveyed my gratitude, perhaps a shade too sharply, borrowed money from a friend, and myself and my lover took the boat to France.

I had never thought of myself as an essayist: the idea had never entered my mind. Even — or, perhaps, especially now — I find it hard to re-create the journey.

It has something to do, certainly, with what I was trying to discover and, also, trying to avoid. If I was trying to discover myself — on the whole, when examined, a somewhat dubious notion, since I was also trying to avoid myself — there was, certainly, between that self and me, the accumulated rock of ages. This rock scarred the hand, and all tools broke against it. Yet, there was a *me*, somewhere: I could feel it, stirring within and against captivity. The hope of salvation — identity — depended on whether or not one would be able to decipher and describe the rock.

One song cries, *"lead me to the rock that is higher than I,"* and another cries, *"hide me in the rock!"* and yet another proclaims, *"I got a home in that rock."* Or, *"I ran to the rock to hide my face: the rock cried out, no hiding place!"*

The accumulated rock of ages deciphered itself as a part of my inheritance — a part, mind you, not the totality — but, in order to claim my birthright, of which my inheritance was but a shadow, it was necessary to challenge and claim the rock. Otherwise, the rock claimed me.

Or, to put it another way, my inheritance was particular, specifically limited and limiting: my birthright was vast, connecting me to all that lives, and to everyone, forever. But one cannot claim the birthright without accepting the inheritance.

Therefore, when I began, seriously, to write — when I knew I was committed, that this would be my life — I had to try to describe that particular condition which was — is — the living proof of my inheritance. And, at the same time, with that very same description, I had to claim my birthright. I am what time, circumstance, history, have made of me, certainly, but I am, also, much more than that. So are we all.

The conundrum of color is the inheritance of every American, be he/she legally or actually Black or White. It is a fearful inheritance, for which untold multitudes, long ago, sold their birthright. Multitudes are doing so, until today. This horror has so welded past and present that it is virtually impossible and certainly meaningless to speak of it as occurring, as it were, in time. It can be, and it has been, suicidal to attempt to speak of this to a multitude, which, assuming it knows that time exists, believes that time can be outwitted.

Something like this, anyway, has something to do with my beginnings. I was trying to locate myself within a specific inheritance and to use that inheritance, precisely, to claim the birthright from which that inheritance had so brutally and specifically excluded me.

It is not pleasant to be forced to recognize, more than thirty years later, that neither this dynamic nor this necessity have changed. There have been superficial changes, with results at best ambiguous and, at worst, disastrous.

Morally, there has been no change at all and a moral change is the only real one. *"Plus ça change,"* groan the exasperated French (who should certainly know), *"plus c'est le même chose."* (The more it changes, the more it remains the same.) At least they have the style to be truthful about it.

The only real change vividly discernible in this present, unspeakably dangerous chaos is a panic-stricken apprehension on the part of those who have maligned and subjugated others for so long that the tables have been turned. Not once have the Civilized been able to honor, recognize, or describe the Savage. He is, practically speaking, the source of their wealth, his continued subjugation the key to their power and glory. This is absolutely and unanswerably true in South Africa — to name but one section of Africa — and, as to how things fare for Black men and women; here, the Black has become, economically, all but expendable and is, therefore, encouraged to join the Army, or, a notion espoused, I believe, by Daniel Moynihan and Nathan Glazer, to become a postman — to make himself useful, for Christ's sake, while White men take on the heavy burden of ruling the world.

Well. *Plus ça change.* To say nothing, speaking as a Black citizen, regarding his countrymen, of *friends like these.*

There is an unadmitted icy panic coiled beneath the scaffolding of these present days, hopes, endeavors. I have said that the Civilized have never been able to honor, recognize, or describe the Savage. Once they had decided that he was savage, there was nothing to honor, recognize or describe. But the savages describe the Europeans, who were not yet, when they landed in the

New(!) World, White, as *the people from heaven*. Neither did the savages in Africa have any way of foreseeing the anguished diaspora to which they were about to be condemned. Even the chiefs who sold Africans into slavery could not have had any idea that this slavery was meant to endure forever, or for at least *a thousand years*. Nothing in the savage experience could have prepared them for such an idea, any more than they could conceive of the land as something to be bought and sold. (As I cannot believe that people are actually buying and selling air space above the towers of Manhattan.)

Nevertheless, all of this happened, and is happening. Out of this incredible brutality, we get the myth of the happy darky and *Gone With the Wind*. And the North Americans appear to believe these legends, which they have created and which absolutely nothing in reality corroborates, until today. And when these legends are attacked, as is happening now — all over a globe which has never been and never will be White — my countrymen become childishly vindictive and unutterably dangerous.

The unadmitted panic of which I spoke above is created by the terror that the Savage can, now, describe the Civilized: the only way to prevent this is to obliterate humanity. This panic proves that neither a person nor a people can do anything without knowing what they are doing. Neither can anyone avoid paying for the choices he or she has made. It is savagely, if one may say so, ironical that the only proof the world — mankind — has ever had of White supremacy is in the Black face and voice: that face never scrutinized, that voice never heard. The eyes in that face prove the unforgivable and un-

imaginable horror of being a captive in the promised land,
but also prove that *trouble don't last always:* and the
voice, once filled with a rage and pain that corroborated
the reality of the jailer, is addressing another reality, in
other tongues. The people who think of themselves as
White have the choice of becoming human or irrelevant.

Or — as they are, indeed, already, in all but actual
fact: obsolete. For, if trouble don't last always, as the
Preacher tells us, neither does Power, and it is on the fact
or the hope or the myth of Power that that identity which
calls itself White has always seemed to depend.

I had just turned thirty-one when this book was first
published, and, by the time you read this, I will be sixty.
I think that quite remarkable, but I do not mention it,
now, as an occasion for celebrations or lamentations. I
don't feel that I have any reason to complain: emphati-
cally, the contrary, to leave it at that, and no matter what
tomorrow brings. Yet, I have reason to reflect — one always does, when forced to take a long look back. I remember many people who helped me in indescribable
ways, all those years ago, when I was the popeyed,
tongue-tied kid, in my memory sitting in a corner, on the
floor. I was having a rough time in the Village, where
the bulk of the populace, egged on by the cops, thought
it was great fun to bounce tables and chairs off my head,
and I soon stopped talking about my "constitutional"
rights. I am, I suppose, a survivor.

A survivor of what? In those years, I was told, when
I became terrified, vehement, or lachrymose: *It takes
time, Jimmy. It takes time.* I agree: I still agree: though
it certainly didn't take much time for some of the people
I knew then — in the Fifties — to turn tail, to decide to

make it, and drape themselves in the American flag. A wretched and despicable band of cowards, whom I once trusted with my life — *friends like these!*

But we will discuss all that another day. When I was told, it takes time, when I was young, I was being told it will take time before a Black person can be treated as a human being here, but it will happen. We will help to make it happen. We promise you.

Sixty years of one man's life is a long time to deliver on a promise, especially considering all the lives preceding and surrounding my own.

What has happened, in the time of my time, is the record of my ancestors. No promise was kept with them, no promise was kept with me, nor can I counsel those coming after me, nor my global kinsmen, to believe a word uttered by my morally bankrupt and desperately dishonest countrymen.

"And," says Doris Lessing, in her preface to *African Stories, "while the cruelties of the white man toward the black man are among the heaviest counts in the indictment against humanity, colour prejudice is not our original fault, but only one aspect of the atrophy of the imagination that prevents us from seeing ourselves in every creature that breathes under the sun."*

Amen. *En avant.*

18 April 1984
Amherst, Massachusetts

NOTES OF A NATIVE SON

Autobiographical Notes

I was born in Harlem thirty-one years ago. I began plotting novels at about the time I learned to read. The story of my childhood is the usual bleak fantasy, and we can dismiss it with the restrained observation that I certainly would not consider living it again. In those days my mother was given to the exasperating and mysterious habit of having babies. As they were born, I took them over with one hand and held a book with the other. The children probably suffered, though they have since been kind enough to deny it, and in this way I read *Uncle Tom's Cabin* and *A Tale of Two Cities* over and over and over again; in this way, in fact, I read just about everything I could get my hands on — except the Bible, probably because it was the only book I was encouraged to read. I must also confess that I wrote — a great deal — and my first professional triumph, in any case, the first effort of mine to be seen in print, occurred at the age of twelve or thereabouts, when a short story I had written about the Spanish revolution won some sort of prize in an extremely short-lived church newspaper. I remember the story was censored by the lady editor, though I don't remember why, and I was outraged.

Also wrote plays, and songs, for one of which I received a letter of congratulations from Mayor La Guardia, and poetry, about which the less said, the better. My mother

3

was delighted by all these goings-on, but my father wasn't; he wanted me to be a preacher. When I was fourteen I became a preacher, and when I was seventeen I stopped. Very shortly thereafter I left home. For God knows how long I struggled with the world of commerce and industry — I guess they would say they struggled with *me* — and when I was about twenty-one I had enough done of a novel to get a Saxton Fellowship. When I was twenty-two the fellowship was over, the novel turned out to be unsalable, and I started waiting on tables in a Village restaurant and writing book reviews — mostly, as it turned out, about the Negro problem, concerning which the color of my skin made me automatically an expert. Did another book, in company with photographer Theodore Pelatowski, about the store-front churches in Harlem. This book met exactly the same fate as my first — fellowship, but no sale. (It was a Rosenwald Fellowship.) By the time I was twenty-four I had decided to stop reviewing books about the Negro problem — which, by this time, was only slightly less horrible in print than it was in life — and I packed my bags and went to France, where I finished, God knows how, *Go Tell It on the Mountain.*

Any writer, I suppose, feels that the world into which he was born is nothing less than a conspiracy against the cultivation of his talent — which attitude certainly has a great deal to support it. On the other hand, it is only because the world looks on his talent with such a frightening indifference that the artist is compelled to make his talent important. So that any writer, looking back over even so short a span of time as I am here forced to assess, finds that the things which hurt him and the things which helped him cannot be divorced from each other; he could be helped in a certain way only because he was hurt in a certain way; and his help is simply to be enabled to move from one conundrum to the next — one is tempted to say that he moves from one disaster to the next. When one begins looking for influences one finds them by the score. I haven't thought much about my own, not enough anyway; I hazard that the King James Bible, the rhetoric of the store-front church, something ironic and violent and perpetually understated in Negro speech — and something of Dickens' love for bravura — have something to do with me today; but I wouldn't stake my life on it. Likewise, innumerable people have helped me in many ways; but finally, I suppose, the most difficult (and most rewarding) thing in my life has been the fact that I was born a Negro and was forced, therefore, to effect some kind of truce with this reality. (Truce, by the way, is the best one can hope for.)

One of the difficulties about being a Negro writer (and this is not special pleading, since I don't mean to suggest that he has it worse than anybody else) is that the Negro problem is written about so widely. The bookshelves groan under the weight of information, and everyone therefore considers himself informed. And this information, furthermore, operates usually (generally, popularly) to reinforce traditional attitudes. Of traditional attitudes there are only two — For or Against — and I, personally, find it difficult to say which attitude has caused me the most pain. I am speaking as a writer; from a social point of view I am perfectly aware that the change from ill-will to good-will, however motivated, however imperfect, however expressed, is better than no change at all.

But it is part of the business of the writer — as I see it

— to examine attitudes, to go beneath the surface, to tap the source. From this point of view the Negro problem is nearly inaccessible. It is not only written about so widely; it is written about so badly. It is quite possible to say that the price a Negro pays for becoming articulate is to find himself, at length, with nothing to be articulate about. ("You taught me language," says Caliban to Prospero, "and my profit on't is I know how to curse.") Consider: the tremendous social activity that this problem generates imposes on whites and Negroes alike the necessity of looking forward, of working to bring about a better day. This is fine, it keeps the waters troubled; it is all, indeed, that has made possible the Negro's progress. Nevertheless, social affairs are not generally speaking the writer's prime concern, whether they ought to be or not; it is absolutely necessary that he establish between himself and these affairs a distance which will allow, at least, for clarity, so that before he can look forward in any meaningful sense, he must first be allowed to take a long look back. In the context of the Negro problem neither whites nor blacks, for excellent reasons of their own, have the faintest desire to look back; but I think that the past is all that makes the present coherent, and further, that the past will remain horrible for exactly as long as we refuse to assess it honestly.

I know, in any case, that the most crucial time in my own development came when I was forced to recognize that I was a kind of bastard of the West; when I followed the line of my past I did not find myself in Europe but in Africa. And this meant that in some subtle way, in a really profound way, I brought to Shakespeare, Bach, Rembrandt, to the stones of Paris, to the cathedral at Chartres, and to the Empire State Building, a special attitude. These were not really my creations, they did not contain my history; I might search in them in vain forever for any reflection of myself. I was an interloper; this was not my heritage. At the same time I had no other heritage which I could possibly hope to use—I had certainly been unfitted for the jungle or the tribe. I would have to appropriate these white centuries, I would have to make them mine — I would have to accept my special attitude, my special place in this scheme — otherwise I would have no place in *any* scheme. What was the most difficult was the fact that I was forced to admit something I had always hidden from myself, which the American Negro has had to hide from himself as the price of his public progress; that I hated and feared white people. This did not mean that I loved black people; on the contrary, I despised them, possibly because they failed to produce Rembrandt. In effect, I hated and feared the world. And this meant, not only that I thus gave the world an altogether murderous power over me, but also that in such a self-destroying limbo I could never hope to write.

One writes out of one thing only — one's own experience. Everything depends on how relentlessly one forces from this experience the last drop, sweet or bitter, it can possibly give. This is the only real concern of the artist, to recreate out of the disorder of life that order which is art. The difficulty then, for me, of being a Negro writer was the fact that I was, in effect, prohibited from examining my own experience too closely by the tremendous demands and the very real dangers of my social situation.

I don't think the dilemma outlined above is uncommon. I do think, since writers work in the disastrously explicit medium of language, that it goes a little way towards explaining why, out of the enormous resources of Negro speech and life, and despite the example of Negro music, prose written by Negroes has been generally speaking so pallid and so harsh. I have not written about being a Negro at such length because I expect that to be my only subject, but only because it was the gate I had to unlock before I could hope to write about anything else. I don't think that the Negro problem in America can be even discussed coherently without bearing in mind its context; its context being the history, traditions, customs, the moral assumptions and preoccupations of the country; in short, the general social fabric. Appearances to the contrary, no one in America escapes its effects and everyone in America bears some responsibility for it. I believe this the more firmly because it is the overwhelming tendency to speak of this problem as though it were a thing apart. But in the work of Faulkner, in the general attitude and certain specific passages in Robert Penn Warren, and, most significantly, in the advent of Ralph Ellison, one sees the beginnings — at least — of a more genuinely penetrating search. Mr. Ellison, by the way, is the first Negro novelist I have ever read to utilize in language, and brilliantly, some of the ambiguity and irony of Negro life.

About my interests: I don't know if I have any, unless the morbid desire to own a sixteen-millimeter camera and make experimental movies can be so classified. Otherwise, I love to eat and drink — it's my melancholy conviction that I've scarcely ever had enough to eat (this is because it's *impossible* to eat enough if you're worried about the next meal) — and I love to argue with people who do not disagree with me too profoundly, and I love to laugh.

I do *not* like bohemia, or bohemians, I do not like people whose principal aim is pleasure, and I do not like people who are *earnest* about anything. I don't like people who like me because I'm a Negro; neither do I like people who find in the same accident grounds for contempt. I love America more than any other country in the world, and, exactly for this reason, I insist on the right to criticize her perpetually. I think all theories are suspect, that the finest principles may have to be modified, or may even be pulverized by the demands of life, and that one must find, therefore, one's own moral center and move through the world hoping that this center will guide one aright. I consider that I have many responsibilities, but none greater than this: to last, as Hemingway says, and get my work done.

I want to be an honest man and a good writer.

PART ONE

Everybody's Protest Novel

In *Uncle Tom's Cabin,* that cornerstone of American social protest fiction, St. Clare, the kindly master, remarks to his coldly disapproving Yankee cousin, Miss Ophelia, that, so far as he is able to tell, the blacks have been turned over to the devil for the benefit of the whites in this world — however, he adds thoughtfully, it may turn out in the next. Miss Ophelia's reaction is, at least, vehemently right-minded: "This is perfectly horrible!" she exclaims. "You ought to be ashamed of yourselves!"

Miss Ophelia, as we may suppose, was speaking for the author; her exclamation is the moral, neatly framed, and incontestable like those improving mottoes sometimes found hanging on the walls of furnished rooms. And, like these mottoes, before which one invariably flinches, recognizing an insupportable, almost an indecent glibness, she and St. Clare are terribly in earnest. Neither of them questions the medieval morality from which their dialogue springs: black, white, the devil, the next world — posing its alternatives between heaven and the flames — were realities for them as, of course, they were for their creator. They spurned and were terrified of the darkness, striving mightily for the light; and considered from this aspect, Miss Ophelia's exclamation, like Mrs. Stowe's novel, achieves a bright, almost a lurid significance, like the light from a fire which consumes a witch. This is the more striking as one considers the novels of Negro oppression written in our own, more enlightened day, all of which say only: "This is perfectly horrible! You ought to be ashamed of yourselves!" (Let us ignore, for the moment, those novels of oppression written by Negroes, which add only a raging, near-paranoiac postscript to this statement and actually reinforce, as I hope to make clear later, the principles which activate the oppression they decry.)

Uncle Tom's Cabin is a very bad novel, having, in its self-righteous, virtuous sentimentality, much in common with *Little Women*. Sentimentality, the ostentatious parading of excessive and spurious emotion, is the mark of dishonesty, the inability to feel; the wet eyes of the sentimentalist betray his aversion to experience, his fear of life, his arid heart; and it is always, therefore, the signal of secret and violent inhumanity, the mask of cruelty. *Uncle Tom's Cabin* — like its multitudinous, hard-boiled descendants — is a catalogue of violence. This is explained by the nature of Mrs. Stowe's subject matter, her laudable determination to flinch from nothing in presenting the complete picture; an explanation which falters only if we pause to ask whether or not her picture is indeed complete; and what constriction or failure of perception forced her to so depend on the description of brutality — unmotivated, senseless — and to leave unanswered and unnoticed the only important question: what it was, after all, that moved her people to such deeds.

But this, let us say, was beyond Mrs. Stowe's powers; she was not so much a novelist as an impassioned pamphleteer; her book was not intended to do anything more than prove that slavery was wrong; was, in fact, perfectly horrible. This makes material for a pamphlet but it is hardly enough for a novel; and the only question left to ask is why we are bound still within the same constriction. How is it that we are so loath to make a further journey than that made by Mrs. Stowe, to discover and reveal something a little closer to the truth?

But that battered word, truth, having made its appearance here, confronts one immediately with a series of riddles and has, moreover, since so many gospels are preached, the unfortunate tendency to make one belligerent. Let us say, then, that truth, as used here, is meant to imply a devotion to the human being, his freedom and fulfillment; freedom which cannot be legislated, fulfillment which cannot be charted. This is the prime concern, the frame of reference; it is not to be confused with a devotion to Humanity which is too easily equated with a devotion to a Cause; and Causes, as we know, are notoriously bloodthirsty. We have, as it seems to me, in this most mechanical and interlocking of civilizations, attempted to lop this creature down to the status of a time-saving invention. He is not, after all, merely a member of a Society or a Group or a deplorable conundrum to be explained by Science. He is — and how old-fashioned the words sound! — something more than that, something resolutely indefinable, unpredictable. In overlooking, denying, evading his complexity — which is nothing more than the disquieting complexity of ourselves — we are diminished and we perish; only within this web of ambiguity, paradox, this hunger, danger, darkness, can we find at once ourselves and the power that will free us from ourselves. It is this power of revelation which is the business of the novelist, this journey toward a more vast reality which must take precedence over all other claims. What is today parroted as his Responsibility — which seems to mean that he must make formal declaration that he is involved in, and affected by, the lives of other people and to say something improving about this somewhat self-evident fact — is, when he believes it, his corruption and our loss; moreover, it is rooted in, interlocked with and intensifies this same mechanization. Both *Gentleman's Agreement* and *The Postman Always Rings Twice* exemplify this terror of the human being, the determination to cut him down to size. And in *Uncle Tom's Cabin* we may find foreshadowing of both: the formula created by the necessity to find a lie more palatable than the truth has been handed down and memorized and persists yet with a terrible power.

It is interesting to consider one more aspect of Mrs. Stowe's novel, the method she used to solve the problem of writing about a black man at all. Apart from her lively procession of field hands, house niggers, Chloe, Topsy, etc. — who are the stock, lovable figures presenting no problem — she has only three other Negroes in the book. These are the important ones and two of them may be dismissed immediately, since we have only the author's word that they are Negro and they are, in all other respects, as white as she can make them. The two are George and Eliza, a married couple with a wholly adorable child — whose quaintness, incidentally, and whose charm, rather put one in mind of a darky bootblack doing a buck and wing to the clatter of condescending coins. Eliza is a beautiful, pious hybrid, light enough to pass — the heroine of *Quality* might, indeed, be her reincarnation — differing from the genteel mistress who has overseered her education only in the respect that she is a servant. George is darker, but makes up for it by being a mechanical genius, and is, moreover, sufficiently un-Negroid to pass through town, a fugitive from his master, disguised as a Spanish gentleman, attracting no attention whatever beyond admiration. They are a race apart from Topsy. It transpires by the end of the novel, through one of those energetic, last-minute convolutions of the plot, that Eliza has some connection with French gentility. The figure from whom the novel takes its name, Uncle Tom, who is a figure of controversy yet, is jet-black, wooly-haired, illiterate; and he is phenomenally forbearing. He has to be; he is black; only through this forbearance can he survive or triumph. (*Cf.* Faulkner's preface to *The Sound and the Fury*: These others were not Compsons. They were black: — They endured.) His triumph is metaphysical, unearthly; since he is black, born without the light, it is only through humility, the incessant mortification of the flesh, that he can enter into communion with God or man. The virtuous rage of Mrs. Stowe is motivated by nothing so temporal as a concern for the relationship of men to one another — or, even, as she would have claimed, by a concern for their relationship to God — but merely by a panic of being hurled into the flames, of being caught in traffic with the devil. She embraced this merciless doctrine with all her heart, bargaining shamelessly before the throne of grace: God and salvation becoming her personal property, purchased with the coin of her virtue. Here, black equates with evil and white with grace; if, being mindful of the necessity of good works, she could not cast out the blacks — a wretched, huddled mass, apparently, claiming, like an obsession, her inner eye — she could not embrace them either without purifying them of sin. She must cover their intimidating nakedness, robe them in white, the garments of salvation; only thus could she herself be delivered from ever-present sin, only thus could she bury, as St. Paul demanded, "the carnal man, the man of the flesh." Tom, therefore, her only black man, has been robbed of his humanity and divested of his sex. It is the price for that darkness with which he has been branded.

Uncle Tom's Cabin, then, is activated by what might be called a theological terror, the terror of damnation; and the spirit that breathes in this book, hot, self-righteous, fearful, is not different from that spirit of medieval times which sought to exorcize evil by burning witches; and is not different from that terror which activates a lynch mob. One need not, indeed, search for examples so historic or so gaudy; this is a warfare waged daily in the heart, a warfare so vast, so relentless and so powerful that the interracial handshake or the interracial marriage can be as crucifying as the public hanging or the secret rape. This panic motivates our cruelty, this fear of the dark makes it impossible that our lives shall be other than superficial; this, interlocked with and feeding our glittering, mechanical, inescapable civilization which has put to death our freedom.

This, notwithstanding that the avowed aim of the American protest novel is to bring greater freedom to the oppressed. They are forgiven, on the strength of these good intentions, whatever violence they do to language, whatever excessive demands they make of credibility. It is, indeed, considered the sign of a frivolity so intense as to approach decadence to suggest that these books are both badly written and wildly improbable. One is told to put first things first, the good of society coming before niceties of style or characterization. Even if this were

incontestable — for what exactly is the "good" of society?
— it argues an insuperable confusion, since literature and
sociology are not one and the same; it is impossible to
discuss them as if they were. Our passion for categorization, life neatly fitted into pegs, has led to an unforeseen,
paradoxical distress; confusion, a breakdown of meaning.
Those categories which were meant to define and control
the world for us have boomeranged us into chaos; in which
limbo we whirl, clutching the straws of our definitions.
The "protest" novel, so far from being disturbing, is an accepted and comforting aspect of the American scene,
ramifying that framework we believe to be so necessary.
Whatever unsettling questions are raised are evanescent,
titillating; remote, for this has nothing to do with us, it is
safely ensconced in the social arena, where, indeed, it has
nothing to do with anyone, so that finally we receive a
very definite thrill of virtue from the fact that we are reading such a book at all. This report from the pit reassures us
of its reality and its darkness and of our own salvation;
and "As long as such books are being published," an American liberal once said to me, "everything will be all right."

But unless one's ideal of society is a race of neatly
analyzed, hard-working ciphers, one can hardly claim for
the protest novels the lofty purpose they claim for themselves or share the present optimism concerning them.
They emerge for what they are: a mirror of our confusion,
dishonesty, panic, trapped and immobilized in the sunlit
prison of the American dream. They are fantasies, connecting nowhere with reality, sentimental; in exactly the
same sense that such movies as *The Best Years of Our
Lives* or the works of Mr. James M. Cain are fantasies.
Beneath the dazzling pyrotechnics of these current operas

one may still discern, as the controlling force, the intense theological preoccupations of Mrs. Stowe, the sick vacuities of *The Rover Boys*. Finally, the aim of the protest novel becomes something very closely resembling the zeal of those alabaster missionaries to Africa to cover the nakedness of the natives, to hurry them into the pallid arms of Jesus and thence into slavery. The aim has now become to reduce all Americans to the compulsive, bloodless dimensions of a guy named Joe.

It is the peculiar triumph of society — and its loss — that it is able to convince those people to whom it has given inferior status of the reality of this decree; it has the force and the weapons to translate its dictum into fact, so that the allegedly inferior are actually made so, insofar as the societal realities are concerned. This is a more hidden phenomenon now than it was in the days of serfdom, but it is no less implacable. Now, as then, we find ourselves bound, first without, then within, by the nature of our categorization. And escape is not effected through a bitter railing against this trap; it is as though this very striving were the only motion needed to spring the trap upon us. We take our shape, it is true, within and against that cage of reality bequeathed us at our birth; and yet it is precisely through our dependence on this reality that we are most endlessly betrayed. Society is held together by our need; we bind it together with legend, myth, coercion, fearing that without it we will be hurled into that void, within which, like the earth before the Word was spoken, the foundations of society are hidden. From this void — ourselves — it is the function of society to protect us; but it is only this void, our unknown selves, demanding, forever, a new act of creation,

which can save us — "from the evil that is in the world."
With the same motion, at the same time, it is this toward
which we endlessly struggle and from which, endlessly,
we struggle to escape.

It must be remembered that the oppressed and the
oppressor are bound together within the same society;
they accept the same criteria, they share the same beliefs,
they both alike depend on the same reality. Within this
cage it is romantic, more, meaningless, to speak of a "new"
society as the desire of the oppressed, for that shivering
dependence on the props of reality which he shares with
the *Herrenvolk* makes a truly "new" society impossible to
conceive. What is meant by a new society is one in which
inequalities will disappear, in which vengeance will be
exacted; either there will be no oppressed at all, or the
oppressed and the oppressor will change places. But,
finally, as it seems to me, what the rejected desire is, is an
elevation of status, acceptance within the present community. Thus, the African, exile, pagan, hurried off the
auction block and into the fields, fell on his knees before
that God in Whom he must now believe; who had made
him, but not in His image. This tableau, this impossibility,
is the heritage of the Negro in America: *Wash me,* cried
the slave to his Maker, *and I shall be whiter, whiter than
snow!* For black is the color of evil; only the robes of the
saved are white. It is this cry, implacable on the air and
in the skull, that he must live with. Beneath the widely
published catalogue of brutality—bringing to mind, somehow, an image, a memory of church-bells burdening the
air — is this reality which, in the same nightmare notion,
he both flees and rushes to embrace. In America, now,
this country devoted to the death of the paradox — which

may, therefore, be put to death by one — his lot is as ambiguous as a tableau by Kafka. To flee or not, to move or not, it is all the same; his doom is written on his forehead, it is carried in his heart. In *Native Son*, Bigger Thomas stands on a Chicago street corner watching airplanes flown by white men racing against the sun and "Goddamn" he says, the bitterness bubbling up like blood, remembering a million indignities, the terrible, rat-infested house, the humiliation of home-relief, the intense, aimless, ugly bickering, hating it; hatred smoulders through these pages like sulphur fire. All of Bigger's life is controlled, defined by his hatred and his fear. And later, his fear drives him to murder and his hatred to rape; he dies, having come, through this violence, we are told, for the first time, to a kind of life, having for the first time redeemed his manhood. Below the surface of this novel there lies, as it seems to me, a continuation, a complement of that monstrous legend it was written to destroy. Bigger is Uncle Tom's descendant, flesh of his flesh, so exactly opposite a portrait that, when the books are placed together, it seems that the contemporary Negro novelist and the dead New England woman are locked together in a deadly, timeless battle; the one uttering merciless exhortations, the other shouting curses. And, indeed, within this web of lust and fury, black and white can only thrust and counter-thrust, long for each other's slow, exquisite death; death by torture, acid, knives and burning; the thrust, the counter-thrust, the longing making the heavier that cloud which blinds and suffocates them both, so that they go down into the pit together. Thus has the cage betrayed us all, this moment, our life, turned to nothing through our terrible attempts to insure it. For Bigger's tragedy is not that he is cold or black or hungry, not even that he is American, black; but that he has accepted a theology that denies him life, that he admits the possibility of his being sub-human and feels constrained, therefore, to battle for his humanity according to those brutal criteria bequeathed him at his birth. But our humanity is our burden, our life; we need not battle for it; we need only to do what is infinitely more difficult — that is, accept it. The failure of the protest novel lies in its rejection of life, the human being, the denial of his beauty, dread, power, in its insistence that it is his categorization alone which is real and which cannot be transcended.

Many Thousands Gone

It is only in his music, which Americans are able to admire because a protective sentimentality limits their understanding of it, that the Negro in America has been able to tell his story. It is a story which otherwise has yet to be told and which no American is prepared to hear. As is the inevitable result of things unsaid, we find ourselves until today oppressed with a dangerous and reverberating silence; and the story is told, compulsively, in symbols and signs, in hieroglyphics; it is revealed in Negro speech and in that of the white majority and in their different frames of reference. The ways in which the Negro has affected the American psychology are betrayed in our popular culture and in our morality; in our estrangement from him is the depth of our estrangement from ourselves. We cannot ask: what do we *really* feel about him — such a question merely opens the gates on chaos. What we really feel about him is involved with all that we feel about everything, about everyone, about ourselves.

The story of the Negro in America is the story of America — or, more precisely, it is the story of Americans. It is not a very pretty story: the story of a people is never very pretty. The Negro in America, gloomily referred to as that shadow which lies athwart our national life, is far more than that. He is a series of shadows, self-created, intertwining, which now we helplessly battle. One may say that the Negro in America does not really exist except in the darkness of our minds.

This is why his history and his progress, his relationship to all other Americans, has been kept in the social arena. He is a social and not a personal or a human problem; to think of him is to think of statistics, slums, rapes, injustices, remote violence; it is to be confronted with an endless cataloguing of losses, gains, skirmishes; it is to feel virtuous, outraged, helpless, as though his continuing status among us were somehow analogous to disease — cancer, perhaps, or tuberculosis — which must be checked, even though it cannot be cured. In this arena the black man acquires quite another aspect from that which he has in life. We do not know what to do with him in life; if he breaks our sociological and sentimental image of him we are panic-stricken and we feel ourselves betrayed. When he violates this image, therefore, he stands in the greatest danger (sensing which, we uneasily suspect that he is very often playing a part for our benefit); and, what is not always so apparent but is equally true, we are then in some danger ourselves — hence our retreat or our blind and immediate retaliation.

Our dehumanization of the Negro then is indivisible from our dehumanization of ourselves: the loss of our own identity is the price we pay for our annulment of his. Time and our own force act as our allies, creating an impossible, a fruitless tension between the traditional master and slave. Impossible and fruitless because, literal and visible as this tension has become, it has nothing to do with reality.

Time has made some changes in the Negro face. Nothing has succeeded in making it exactly like our own, though the general desire seems to be to make it blank if one cannot make it white. When it has become blank, the past as thoroughly washed from the black face as it has been from ours, our guilt will be finished — at least it will have ceased to be visible, which we imagine to be much the same thing. But, paradoxically, it is we who prevent this from happening; since it is we, who, every hour that we live, reinvest the black face with our guilt; and we do this — by a further paradox, no less ferocious — helplessly, passionately, out of an unrealized need to suffer absolution.

Today, to be sure, we know that the Negro is not biologically or mentally inferior; there is no truth in those rumors of his body odor or his incorrigible sexuality; or no more truth than can be easily explained or even defended by the social sciences. Yet, in our most recent war, his blood was segregated as was, for the most part, his person. Up to today we are set at a division, so that he may not marry our daughters or our sisters, nor may he — for the most part — eat at our tables or live in our houses. Moreover, those who do, do so at the grave expense of a double alienation: from their own people, whose fabled attributes they must either deny or, worse, cheapen and bring to market; from us, for we require of them, when we accept them, that they at once cease to be Negroes and yet not fail to remember what being a Negro means — to remember, that is, what it means to us. The threshold of insult is higher or lower, according to the people involved, from the bootblack in Atlanta to the celebrity in New York. One must travel very far, among saints with nothing to gain or outcasts with nothing to lose, to find a place where it does not matter — and per-

haps a word or a gesture or simply a silence will testify
that it matters even there.

For it means something to be a Negro, after all, as it
means something to have been born in Ireland or in China,
to live where one sees space and sky or to live where one
sees nothing but rubble or nothing but high buildings.
We cannot escape our origins, however hard we try, those
origins which contain the key — could we but find it —
to all that we later become. What it means to be a Negro
is a good deal more than this essay can discover; what it
means to be a Negro in America can perhaps be suggested
by an examination of the myths we perpetuate about him.

Aunt Jemima and Uncle Tom are dead, their places
taken by a group of amazingly well-adjusted young men
and women, almost as dark, but ferociously literate, well-
dressed and scrubbed, who are never laughed at, who are
not likely ever to set foot in a cotton or tobacco field or
in any but the most modern of kitchens. There are others
who remain, in our odd idiom, "underprivileged"; some
are bitter and these come to grief; some are unhappy,
but, continually presented with the evidence of a better
day soon to come, are speedily becoming less so. Most of
them care nothing whatever about race. They want only
their proper place in the sun and the right to be left alone,
like any other citizen of the republic. We may all breathe
more easily. Before, however, our joy at the demise of
Aunt Jemima and Uncle Tom approaches the indecent, we
had better ask whence they sprang, how they lived? Into
what limbo have they vanished?

However inaccurate our portraits of them were, these
portraits do suggest, not only the conditions, but the quality of their lives and the impact of this spectacle on our

consciences. There was no one more forbearing than
Aunt Jemima, no one stronger or more pious or more loyal
or more wise; there was, at the same time, no one weaker
or more faithless or more vicious and certainly no one
more immoral. Uncle Tom, trustworthy and sexless,
needed only to drop the title "Uncle" to become violent,
crafty, and sullen, a menace to any white woman who
passed by. They prepared our feast tables and our burial
clothes; and, if we could boast that we understood them,
it was far more to the point and far more true that they
understood us. They were, moreover, the only people in
the world who did; and not only did they know us better
than we knew ourselves, but they knew us better than we
knew them. This was the piquant flavoring to the national
joke, it lay behind our uneasiness as it lay behind our
benevolence: Aunt Jemima and Uncle Tom, our creations,
at the last evaded us; they had a life — their own, perhaps
a better life than ours — and they would never tell us
what it was. At the point where we were driven most
privately and painfully to conjecture what depths of contempt, what heights of indifference, what prodigies of
resilience, what untamable superiority allowed them so
vividly to endure, neither perishing nor rising up in a body
to wipe us from the earth, the image perpetually shattered
and the word failed. The black man in our midst carried
murder in his heart, he wanted vengeance. We carried
murder too, we wanted peace.

In our image of the Negro breathes the past we deny,
not dead but living yet and powerful, the beast in our
jungle of statistics. It is this which defeats us, which continues to defeat us, which lends to interracial cocktail
parties their rattling, genteel, nervously smiling air: in any

drawing room at such a gathering the beast may spring, filling the air with flying things and an unenlightened wailing. Wherever the problem touches there is confusion, there is danger. Wherever the Negro face appears a tension is created, the tension of a silence filled with things unutterable. It is a sentimental error, therefore, to believe that the past is dead; it means nothing to say that it is all forgotten, that the Negro himself has forgotten it. It is not a question of memory. Oedipus did not remember the thongs that bound his feet; nevertheless the marks they left testified to that doom toward which his feet were leading him. The man does not remember the hand that struck him, the darkness that frightened him, as a child; nevertheless, the hand and the darkness remain with him, indivisible from himself forever, part of the passion that drives him wherever he thinks to take flight.

The making of an American begins at that point where he himself rejects all other ties, any other history, and himself adopts the vesture of his adopted land. This problem has been faced by all Americans throughout our history — in a way it *is* our history — and it baffles the immigrant and sets on edge the second generation until today. In the case of the Negro the past was taken from him whether he would or no; yet to forswear it was meaningless and availed him nothing, since his shameful history was carried, quite literally, on his brow. Shameful; for he was heathen as well as black and would never have discovered the healing blood of Christ had not we braved the jungles to bring him these glad tidings. Shameful; for, since our role as missionary had not been wholly disinterested, it was necessary to recall the shame from which we had delivered him in order more easily to escape our own. As he accepted the alabaster Christ and the bloody cross — in the bearing of which he would find his redemption, as, indeed, to our outraged astonishment, he sometimes did — he must, henceforth, accept that image we then gave him of himself: having no other and standing, moreover, in danger of death should he fail to accept the dazzling light thus brought into such darkness. It is this quite simple dilemma that must be borne in mind if we wish to comprehend his psychology.

However we shift the light which beats so fiercely on his head, or *prove*, by victorious social analysis, how his lot has changed, how we have both improved, our uneasiness refuses to be exorcized. And nowhere is this more apparent than in our literature on the subject — "problem" literature when written by whites, "protest" literature when written by Negroes — and nothing is more striking than the tremendous disparity of tone between the two creations. *Kingsblood Royal* bears, for example, almost no kinship to *If He Hollers Let Him Go*, though the same reviewers praised them both for what were, at bottom, very much the same reasons. These reasons may be suggested, far too briefly but not at all unjustly, by observing that the presupposition is in both novels exactly the same: black is a terrible color with which to be born into the world.

Now the most powerful and celebrated statement we have yet had of what it means to be a Negro in America is unquestionably Richard Wright's *Native Son*. The feeling which prevailed at the time of its publication was that such a novel, bitter, uncompromising, shocking, gave proof, by its very existence, of what strides might be taken in a free democracy; and its indisputable success, proof that Americans were now able to look full in the face without flinching the dreadful facts. Americans, unhappily, have the most remarkable ability to alchemize all bitter truths into an innocuous but piquant confection and to transform their moral contradictions, or public discussion of such contradictions, into a proud decoration, such as are given for heroism on the field of battle. Such a book, we felt with pride, could never have been written before — which was true. Nor could it be written today. It bears already the aspect of a landmark; for Bigger and his brothers have undergone yet another metamorphosis; they have been accepted in baseball leagues and by colleges hitherto exclusive; and they have made a most favorable appearance on the national screen. We have yet to encounter, nevertheless, a report so indisputably authentic, or one that can begin to challenge this most significant novel.

It is, in a certain American tradition, the story of an unremarkable youth in battle with the force of circumstance; that force of circumstance which plays and which has played so important a part in the national fables of success or failure. In this case the force of circumstance is not poverty merely but color, a circumstance which cannot be overcome, against which the protagonist battles for his life and loses. It is, on the surface, remarkable that this book should have enjoyed among Americans the favor it did enjoy; no more remarkable, however, than that it should have been compared, exuberantly, to Dostoevsky, though placed a shade below Dos Passos, Dreiser, and

Steinbeck; and when the book is examined, its impact does not seem remarkable at all, but becomes, on the contrary, perfectly logical and inevitable.

We cannot, to begin with, divorce this book from the specific social climate of that time: it was one of the last of those angry productions, encountered in the late twenties and all through the thirties, dealing with the inequities of the social structure of America. It was published one year before our entry into the last world war — which is to say, very few years after the dissolution of the WPA and the end of the New Deal and at a time when bread lines and soup kitchens and bloody industrial battles were bright in everyone's memory. The rigors of that unexpected time filled us not only with a genuinely bewildered and despairing idealism — so that, because there at least was *something* to fight for, young men went off to die in Spain — but also with a genuinely bewildered self-consciousness. The Negro, who had been during the magnificent twenties a passionate and delightful primitive, now became, as one of the things we were most self-conscious about, our most oppressed minority. In the thirties, swallowing Marx whole, we discovered the Worker and realized — I should think with some relief — that the aims of the Worker and the aims of the Negro were one. This theorem — to which we shall return — seems now to leave rather too much out of account; it became, nevertheless, one of the slogans of the "class struggle" and the gospel of the New Negro.

As for this New Negro, it was Wright who became his most eloquent spokesman; and his work, from its beginning, is most clearly committed to the social struggle. Leaving aside the considerable question of what relationship precisely the artist bears to the revolutionary, the reality of man as a social being is not his only reality and that artist is strangled who is forced to deal with human beings solely in social terms; and who has, moreover, as Wright had, the necessity thrust on him of being the representative of some thirteen million people. It is a false responsibility (since writers are not congressmen) and impossible, by its nature, of fulfillment. The unlucky shepherd soon finds that, so far from being able to feed the hungry sheep, he has lost the wherewithal for his own nourishment: having not been allowed — so fearful was his burden, so present his audience! — to recreate his own experience. Further, the militant men and women of the thirties were not, upon examination, significantly emancipated from their antecedents, however bitterly they might consider themselves estranged or however gallantly they struggled to build a better world. However they might extol Russia, their concept of a better world was quite helplessly American and betrayed a certain thinness of imagination, a suspect reliance on suspect and badly digested formulae, and a positively fretful romantic haste. Finally, the relationship of the Negro to the Worker cannot be summed up, nor even greatly illuminated, by saying that their aims are one. It is true only insofar as they both desire better working conditions and useful only insofar as they unite their strength as workers to achieve these ends. Further than this we cannot in honesty go.

In this climate Wright's voice first was heard and the struggle which promised for a time to shape his work and give it purpose also fixed it in an ever more unrewarding rage. Recording his days of anger he has also nevertheless recorded, as no Negro before him had ever done, that fantasy Americans hold in their minds when they speak of the Negro: that fantastic and fearful image which we have lived with since the first slave fell beneath the lash. This is the significance of *Native Son* and also, unhappily, its overwhelming limitation.

Native Son begins with the *Brring!* of an alarm clock in the squalid Chicago tenement where Bigger and his family live. Rats live there too, feeding off the garbage, and we first encounter Bigger in the act of killing one. One may consider that the entire book, from that harsh *Brring!* to Bigger's weak "Good-by" as the lawyer, Max, leaves him in the death cell, is an extension, with the roles inverted, of this chilling metaphor. Bigger's situation and Bigger himself exert on the mind the same sort of fascination. The premise of the book is, as I take it, clearly conveyed in these first pages: we are confronting a monster created by the American republic and we are, through being made to share his experience, to receive illumination as regards the manner of his life and to feel both pity and horror at his awful and inevitable doom. This is an arresting and potentially rich idea and we would be discussing a very different novel if Wright's execution had been more perceptive and if he had not attempted to redeem a symbolical monster in social terms.

One may object that it was precisely Wright's intention to create in Bigger a social symbol, revelatory of social disease and prophetic of disaster. I think, however, that it is this assumption which we ought to examine more carefully. Bigger has no discernible relationship to himself, to his own life, to his own people, nor to any other people — in this respect, perhaps, he is most American —

and his force comes, not from his significance as a social
(or anti-social) unit, but from his significance as the
incarnation of a myth. It is remarkable that, though we
follow him step by step from the tenement room to the
death cell, we know as little about him when this journey
is ended as we did when it began; and, what is even more
remarkable, we know almost as little about the social
dynamic which we are to believe created him. Despite
the details of slum life which we are given, I doubt that
anyone who has thought about it, disengaging himself
from sentimentality, can accept this most essential premise
of the novel for a moment. Those Negroes who surround
him, on the other hand, his hard-working mother, his
ambitious sister, his poolroom cronies, Bessie, might be
considered as far richer and far more subtle and accurate
illustrations of the ways in which Negroes are controlled
in our society and the complex techniques they have
evolved for their survival. We are limited, however, to
Bigger's view of them, part of a deliberate plan which
might not have been disastrous if we were not also limited
to Bigger's perceptions. What this means for the novel
is that a necessary dimension has been cut away; this
dimension being the relationship that Negroes bear to one
another, that depth of involvement and unspoken recognition of shared experience which creates a way of life.
What the novel reflects — and at no point interprets — is
the isolation of the Negro within his own group and the
resulting fury of impatient scorn. It is this which creates
its climate of anarchy and unmotivated and unappre-
hended disaster; and it is this climate, common to most
Negro protest novels, which has led us all to believe that
in Negro life there exists no tradition, no field of manners,

no possibility of ritual or intercourse, such as may, for example, sustain the Jew even after he has left his father's house. But the fact is not that the Negro has no tradition but that there has as yet arrived no sensibility sufficiently profound and tough to make this tradition articulate. For a tradition expresses, after all, nothing more than the long and painful experience of a people; it comes out of the battle waged to maintain their integrity or, to put it more simply, out of their struggle to survive. When we speak of the Jewish tradition we are speaking of centuries of exile and persecution, of the strength which endured and the sensibility which discovered in it the high possibility of the moral victory.

This sense of how Negroes live and how they have so long endured is hidden from us in part by the very speed of the Negro's public progress, a progress so heavy with complexity, so bewildering and kaleidoscopic, that he dare not pause to conjecture on the darkness which lies behind him; and by the nature of the American psychology which, in order to apprehend or be made able to accept it, must undergo a metamorphosis so profound as to be literally unthinkable and which there is no doubt we will resist until we are compelled to achieve our own identity by the rigors of a time that has yet to come. Bigger, in the meanwhile, and all his furious kin, serve only to whet the notorious national taste for the sensational and to reinforce all that we now find it necessary to believe. It is not Bigger whom we fear, since his appearance among us makes our victory certain. It is the others, who smile, who go to church, who give no cause for complaint, whom we sometimes consider with amusement, with pity, even with affection — and in whose faces we sometimes surprise the merest arrogant hint of hatred, the faintest, with-drawn, speculative shadow of contempt — who make us uneasy; whom we cajole, threaten, flatter, fear; who to us remain unknown, though we are not (we feel with both relief and hostility and with bottomless confusion) un-known to them. It is out of our reaction to these hewers of wood and drawers of water that our image of Bigger was created.

It is this image, living yet, which we perpetually seek to evade with good works; and this image which makes of all our good works an intolerable mockery. The "nigger," black, benighted, brutal, consumed with hatred as we are consumed with guilt, cannot be thus blotted out. He stands at our shoulders when we give our maid her wages, it is his hand which we fear we are taking when struggling to communicate with the current "intelligent" Negro, his stench, as it were, which fills our mouths with salt as the monument is unveiled in honor of the latest Negro leader. Each generation has shouted behind him, *Nigger!* as he walked our streets; it is he whom we would rather our sisters did not marry; he is banished into the vast and wailing outer darkness whenever we speak of the "purity" of our women, of the "sanctity" of our homes, of "Ameri-can" ideals. What is more, he knows it. He is indeed the "native son": he is the "nigger." Let us refrain from inquiring at the moment whether or not he actually exists; for we *believe* that he exists. Whenever we encounter him amongst us in the flesh, our faith is made perfect and his necessary and bloody end is executed with a mystical ferocity of joy.

But there is a complementary faith among the damned which involves their gathering of the stones with which those who walk in the light shall stone them; or there exists among the intolerably degraded the perverse and powerful desire to force into the arena of the actual those fantastic crimes of which they have been accused, achieving their vengeance and their own destruction through making the nightmare real. The American image of the Negro lives also in the Negro's heart; and when he has surrendered to this image life has no other possible reality. Then he, like the white enemy with whom he will be locked one day in mortal struggle, has no means save this of asserting his identity. This is why Bigger's murder of Mary can be referred to as an "act of creation" and why, once this murder has been committed, he can feel for the first time that he is living fully and deeply as a man was meant to live. And there is, I should think, no Negro living in America who has not felt, briefly or for long periods, with anguish sharp or dull, in varying degrees and to varying effect, simple, naked and unanswerable hatred; who has not wanted to smash any white face he may encounter in a day, to violate, out of motives of the cruelest vengeance, their women, to break the bodies of all white people and bring them low, as low as that dust into which he himself has been and is being trampled; no Negro, finally, who has not had to make his own precarious adjustment to the "nigger" who surrounds him and to the "nigger" in himself.

Yet the adjustment must be made — rather, it must be attempted, the tension perpetually sustained — for without this he has surrendered his birthright as a man no less than his birthright as a black man. The entire universe is then peopled only with his enemies, who are not only white men armed with rope and rifle, but his own far-flung

and contemptible kinsmen. Their blackness is his deg-
radation and it is their stupid and passive endurance
which makes his end inevitable.

Bigger dreams of some black man who will weld all
blacks together into a mighty fist, and feels, in relation to
his family, that perhaps they had to live as they did
precisely because none of them had ever done anything,
right or wrong, which mattered very much. It is only he
who, by an act of murder, has burst the dungeon cell. He
has made it manifest that *he* lives and that his despised
blood nourishes the passions of a man. He has forced his
oppressors to see the fruit of that oppression: and he feels,
when his family and his friends come to visit him in the
death cell, that they should not be weeping or frightened,
that they should be happy, *proud* that he has dared,
through murder and now through his own imminent
destruction, to redeem their anger and humiliation, that
he has hurled into the spiritless obscurity of their lives the
lamp of his passionate life and death. Henceforth, they
may remember Bigger — who has died, as we may conclude, for them. But they do not feel this; they only know
that he has murdered two women and precipitated a
reign of terror; and that now he is to die in the electric
chair. They therefore weep and are honestly frightened
— for which Bigger despises them and wishes to "blot"
them out. What is missing in his situation and in the
representation of his psychology — which makes his situation false and his psychology incapable of development —
is any revelatory apprehension of Bigger as one of the
Negro's realities or as one of the Negro's roles. This failure
is part of the previously noted failure to convey any sense
of Negro life as a continuing and complex group reality.

Bigger, who cannot function therefore as a reflection of
the social illness, having, as it were, no society to reflect,
likewise refuses to function on the loftier level of the
Christ-symbol. His kinsmen are quite right to weep and
be frightened, even to be appalled: for it is not his love
for them or for himself which causes him to die, but his
hatred and his self-hatred; he does not redeem the pains
of a despised people, but reveals, on the contrary, nothing
more than his own fierce bitterness at having been born
one of them. In this also he is the "native son," his progress determinable by the speed with which the distance
increases between himself and the auction-block and all
that the auction-block implies. To have penetrated this
phenomenon, this inward contention of love and hatred,
blackness and whiteness, would have given him a stature
more nearly human and an end more nearly tragic; and
would have given us a document more profoundly and
genuinely bitter and less harsh with an anger which is, on
the one hand, exhibited and, on the other hand, denied.

Native Son finds itself at length so trapped by the
American image of Negro life and by the American necessity to find the ray of hope that it cannot pursue its own
implications. This is why Bigger must be at the last redeemed, to be received, if only by rhetoric, into that community of phantoms which is our tenaciously held ideal of
the happy social life. It is the socially conscious whites
who receive him — the Negroes being capable of no such
objectivity — and we have, by way of illustration, that
lamentable scene in which Jan, Mary's lover, forgives him
for her murder; and, carrying the explicit burden of the
novel, Max's long speech to the jury. This speech, which

really ends the book, is one of the most desperate performances in American fiction. It is the question of Bigger's humanity which is at stake, the relationship in which he stands to all other Americans — and, by implication, to all people — and it is precisely this question which it cannot clarify, with which it cannot, in fact, come to any coherent terms. He is the monster created by the American republic, the present awful sum of generations of oppression; but to say that he is a monster is to fall into the trap of making him subhuman and he must, therefore, be made representative of a way of life which is real and human in precise ratio to the degree to which it seems to us monstrous and strange. It seems to me that this idea carries, implicitly, a most remarkable confession: that is, that Negro life is in fact as debased and impoverished as our theology claims; and, further, that the use to which Wright puts this idea can only proceed from the assumption—not entirely unsound—that Americans, who evade, so far as possible, all genuine experience, have therefore no way of assessing the experience of others and no way of establishing themselves in relation to any way of life which is not their own. The privacy or obscurity of Negro life makes that life capable, in our imaginations, of producing anything at all; and thus the idea of Bigger's monstrosity can be presented without fear of contradiction, since no American has the knowledge or authority to contest it and no Negro has the voice. It is an idea, which, in the framework of the novel, is dignified by the possibility it promptly affords of presenting Bigger as the herald of disaster, the danger signal of a more bitter time to come when not Bigger alone but all his kindred will

rise, in the name of the many thousands who have perished in fire and flood and by rope and torture, to demand
their rightful vengeance.

But it is not quite fair, it seems to me, to exploit the
national innocence in this way. The idea of Bigger as a
warning boomerangs not only because it is quite beyond
the limit of probability that Negroes in America will ever
achieve the means of wreaking vengeance upon the state
but also because it cannot be said that they have any
desire to do so. *Native Son* does not convey the altogether
savage paradox of the American Negro's situation, of
which the social reality which we prefer with such hopeful
superficiality to study is but, as it were, the shadow. It
is not simply the relationship of oppressed to oppressor,
of master to slave, nor is it motivated merely by hatred;
it is also, literally and morally, a *blood* relationship, perhaps the most profound reality of the American experience,
and we cannot begin to unlock it until we accept how
very much it contains of the force and anguish and terror
of love.

Negroes are Americans and their destiny is the country's
destiny. They have no other experience besides their experience on this continent and it is an experience which
cannot be rejected, which yet remains to be embraced.
If, as I believe, no American Negro exists who does not
have his private Bigger Thomas living in the skull, then
what most significantly fails to be illuminated here is the
paradoxical adjustment which is perpetually made, the
Negro being compelled to accept the fact that this dark
and dangerous and unloved stranger is part of himself
forever. Only this recognition sets him in any wise free
and it is this, this necessary ability to contain and even, in

the most honorable sense of the word, to *exploit* the "nigger," which lends to Negro life its high element of the ironic and which causes the most well-meaning of their American critics to make such exhilarating errors when attempting to understand them. To present Bigger as a warning is simply to reinforce the American guilt and fear concerning him, it is most forcefully to limit him to that previously mentioned social arena in which he has no human validity, it is simply to condemn him to death. For he has always been a warning, he represents the evil, the sin and suffering which we are compelled to reject. It is useless to say to the courtroom in which this heathen sits on trial that he is their responsibility, their creation, and his crimes are theirs; and that they ought, therefore, to allow him to live, to make articulate to himself behind the walls of prison the meaning of his existence. The meaning of his existence has already been most adequately expressed, nor does anyone wish, particularly not in the name of democracy, to think of it any more; as for the possibility of articulation, it is this possibility which above all others we most dread. Moreover, the courtroom, judge, jury, witnesses and spectators, recognize immediately that Bigger is their creation and they recognize this not only with hatred and fear and guilt and the resulting fury of self-righteousness but also with that morbid fullness of pride mixed with horror with which one regards the extent and power of one's wickedness. They know that death is his portion, that he runs to death; coming from darkness and dwelling in darkness, he must be, as often as he rises, banished, lest the entire planet be engulfed. And they know, finally, that they do not wish to forgive him and that he does not wish to be forgiven; that he dies, hating them, scorning that appeal which they cannot make to that irrecoverable humanity of his which cannot hear it; and that he *wants* to die because he glories in his hatred and prefers, like Lucifer, rather to rule in hell than serve in heaven.

For, bearing in mind the premise on which the life of such a man is based, *i.e.*, that black is the color of damnation, this is his only possible end. It is the only death which will allow him a kind of dignity or even, however horribly, a kind of beauty. To tell this story, no more than a single aspect of the story of the "nigger," is inevitably and richly to become involved with the force of life and legend, how each perpetually assumes the guise of the other, creating that dense, many-sided and shifting reality which is the world we live in and the world we make. To tell his story is to begin to liberate us from his image and it is, for the first time, to clothe this phantom with flesh and blood, to deepen, by our understanding of him and his relationship to us, our understanding of ourselves and of all men.

But this is not the story which *Native Son* tells, for we find here merely, repeated in anger, the story which we have told in pride. Nor, since the implications of this anger are evaded, are we ever confronted with the actual or potential significance of our pride; which is why we fall, with such a positive glow of recognition, upon Max's long and bitter summing up. It is addressed to those among us of good will and it seems to say that, though there are whites and blacks among us who hate each other, we will not; there are those who are betrayed by greed, by guilt, by blood lust, but not we; we will set our faces against them and join hands and walk together into that dazzling future when there will be no white or black. This is the dream of all liberal men, a dream not at all dishonorable, but, nevertheless, a dream. For, let us join hands on this mountain as we may, the battle is elsewhere. It proceeds far from us in the heat and horror and pain of life itself where all men are betrayed by greed and guilt and blood-lust and where no one's hands are clean. Our good will, from which we yet expect such power to transform us, is thin, passionless, strident: its roots, examined, lead us back to our forebears, whose assumption it was that the black man, to become truly human and acceptable, must first become like us. This assumption once accepted, the Negro in America can only acquiesce in the obliteration of his own personality, the distortion and debasement of his own experience, surrendering to those forces which reduce the person to anonymity and which make themselves manifest daily all over the darkening world.

Carmen Jones: The Dark Is Light Enough

Hollywood's peculiar ability to milk, so to speak, the cow and the goat at the same time — and then to peddle the results as ginger ale — has seldom produced anything more arresting than the 1955 production of *Carmen Jones*. In Hollywood, for example, immorality and evil (which are synonyms in that lexicon) are always vividly punished, though it is the way of the transgressor — hard perhaps but far from unattractive — which keeps us on the edge of our seats, and the transgressor himself (or herself) who engages all our sympathy. Similarly, in *Carmen Jones*, the implicit parallel between an amoral Gypsy and an amoral Negro woman is the entire root idea of the show; but at the same time, bearing in mind the distances covered since *The Birth of a Nation*, it is important that the movie always be able to repudiate any suggestion that Negroes are amoral — which it can only do, considering the role of the Negro in the national psyche, by repudiating any suggestion that Negroes are not white. With a story like *Carmen* interpreted by a Negro cast this may seem a difficult assignment, but Twentieth Century-Fox has brought it off. At the same time they have also triumphantly *not* brought it off, that is to say that the story

46

does deal with amoral people, Carmen *is* a baggage, and it *is* a Negro cast.

This is made possible in the first place, of course, by the fact that *Carmen* is a "classic" or a "work of art" or something, therefore, sacrosanct and, luckily, quite old: it is as ludicrously unenlightened to accuse Mérimée and Bizet of having dirty minds as it is impossible to accuse them of being anti-Negro. (Though it *is* possible perhaps to accuse them of not knowing much and caring less about Gypsies.) In the second place the music helps, for it has assuredly never sounded so bald, or been sung so badly, or had less relevance to life, anybody's life, than in this production. The lyrics, too, in their way, help, being tasteless and vulgar in a way, if not to a degree, which cannot be called characteristic of Negroes. The movie's lifeless unreality is only occasionally threatened by Pearl Bailey, who has, however, been forestalled by Mr. Preminger's direction and is reduced — in a series of awful costumes, designed, it would appear, to camouflage her personality — to doing what is certainly the best that can be done with an abomination called *Beat Out That Rhythm on a Drum* and delivering her lines for the rest of the picture with such a murderously amused disdain that one cannot quite avoid the suspicion that she is commenting on the film. For a second or so at a time she escapes the film's deadly inertia and in Miss Bailey one catches glimpses of the imagination which might have exploded this movie into something worth seeing.

But this movie, more than any movie I can remember having seen, cannot afford, dare not risk, imagination. The "sexiness," for example, of Dorothy Dandridge, who plays Carmen, becomes quite clearly manufactured and even rather silly the moment Pearl Bailey stands anywhere near her.* And the moment one wishes that Pearl Bailey were playing Carmen one understands that *Carmen Jones* is controlled by another movie which Hollywood was studiously *not* making. For, while it is amusing to parallel Bizet's amoral Gypsy with a present-day, lower-class Negro woman, it is a good deal less amusing to parallel the Bizet violence with the violence of the Negro ghetto.

To avoid this — to exploit, that is, Carmen as a brown-skinned baggage but to avoid even suggesting any of the motivations such a present-day Carmen might have — it was helpful, first of all, that the script failed to require the services of any white people. This seals the action off, as it were, in a vacuum in which the spectacle of color is divested of its danger. The color itself then becomes a kind of vacuum which each spectator will fill with his own fantasies. But *Carmen Jones* does not inhabit the never-never land of such bogus but rather entertaining works as *Stormy Weather* or *Cabin in the Sky* — in which at least one could listen to the music; *Carmen Jones* has moved into a stratosphere rather more interesting and more pernicious, in which even Negro speech is parodied out of its charm and liberalized, if one may so put it, out of its force and precision. The result is not that the characters

---

* I have singled out Miss Bailey because the quality of her personality, forthright and wry, and with the authoritative ring of authenticity, highlights for me the lack of any of these qualities, or any positive qualities at all, in the movie itself. She is also the only performer with whose work I am more or less familiar. Since even she is so thoroughly handicapped by the peculiar necessities of *Carmen Jones,* I should like to make it clear that, in discussing the rest of the cast, I am not trying to judge their professional competence, which, on the basis of this movie — they do not even sing in their own voices — it would be quite unfair to

sound like everybody else, which would be bad enough; the result is that they sound ludicrously false and affected, like ante-bellum Negroes imitating their masters. This is also the way they look, and also rather the way they are dressed, and the word that springs immediately to mind to describe the appallingly technicolored sets — an army camp, a room, and a street on Chicago's South Side, presumably, which Bigger Thomas would certainly fail to recognize — is "spotless." They could easily have been dreamed up by someone determined to prove that Negroes are as "clean" and as "modern" as white people and, I suppose, in one way or another, that is exactly how they *were* dreamed up.

And one is not allowed to forget for an instant that one is watching an opera (a word apparently synonymous in Mr. Preminger's mind with tragedy *and* fantasy), and the tone of *Carmen Jones* is stifling: a wedding of the blank, lofty solemnity with which Hollywood so often approaches "works of art" and the really quite helpless condescension with which Hollywood has always handled Negroes. The fact that one is watching a Negro cast interpreting *Carmen* is used to justify their remarkable vacuity, their complete improbability, their total divorce from anything suggestive of the realities of Negro life. On the other hand, the movie cannot possibly avoid depending very heavily on a certain quaintness, a certain lack of inhibition taken to be typical of Negroes, and further, the exigencies of the story — to say nothing of the images, which we will discuss in a moment — make it necessary to watch this movie, holding in the mind three disparate ideas: (1) that this is an opera having nothing to do with the present day, hence, nothing, *really*, to do with Negroes; but (2) the greater passion, that winning warmth (of which the movie exhibits not a trace), so typical of Negroes makes *Carmen* an ideal vehicle for their graduation into Art; and (3) these are *exceptional* Negroes, as American, that is, as you and me, interpreting lower-class Negroes of whom they, also, are very fond, an affection which is proven perhaps by the fact that everyone appears to undergo a tiny, strangling death before resolutely substituting "de" for "the."

A movie is, literally, a series of images, and what one *sees* in a movie can really be taken, beyond its stammering or misleading dialogue, as the key to what the movie is actually involved in saying. *Carmen Jones* is one of the first and most explicit — and far and away the most self-conscious — weddings of sex and color which Hollywood has yet turned out. (It will most certainly not be the last.) From this point of view the color wheel in *Carmen Jones* is very important. Dorothy Dandridge — Carmen — is a sort of taffy-colored girl, very obviously and vividly dressed, but really in herself rather more sweet than vivid. One feels — perhaps one is meant to feel — that here is a *very* nice girl making her way in movies by means of a bad-girl part; and the glow thus caused, especially since she is a colored girl, really must make up for the glow which is missing from the performance she is clearly working very hard at. Harry Belafonte is just a little darker and just as blankly handsome and fares very badly opposite her in a really offensive version of an already unendurable role. Olga James is Micaela, here called Cindy Lou, a much paler girl than Miss Dandridge but also much plainer, who is compelled to go through the entire movie in a kind of tearful stoop. Joe Adams is Husky Miller

(Escamillo) and he is also rather taffy-colored, but since he is the second lead and by way of being the villain, he is not required to be as blank as Mr. Belafonte and there is therefore, simply in his presence, some fleeting hint of masculine or at least boyish force. For the rest, Pearl Bailey is quite dark and she plays, in effect, a floozie. The wicked sergeant who causes Joe to desert the army — in one of many wildly improbable scenes — and who has evil designs on Carmen is very dark indeed; and so is Husky Miller's trainer, who is, one is given to suppose, Miss Bailey's sugar-daddy. It is quite clear that these people do not live in the same world with Carmen, or Joe, or Cindy Lou. All three of the leads are presented as indefinably complex and tragic, not after money or rhinestones but something else which causes them to be misunderstood by the more earthy types around them. This something else is love, of course, and it is with the handling of this love story that the movie really goes to town.

It is true that no one in the original *Carmen*, least of all Carmen and her lover, are very clearly motivated; but there it scarcely matters because the opera is able to get by on a purely theatrical excitement, a sort of papier-mâché violence, and the intense, if finally incredible, sexuality of its heroine. The movie does not have any of this to work with, since here excitement or violence could only blow the movie to bits, and, while the movie certainly indicates that Carmen is a luscious lollipop, it is on rather more uncertain ground when confronted with the notion of how attractive *she* finds men, and it cannot, in any case, use this as a motivating factor. Carmen is thus robbed at a stroke of even her fake vitality and all her cohesiveness and has become, instead, a nice girl, if a little fiery, whose great fault — and, since this is a tragedy, also her triumph — is that she looks at "life," as her final aria states it, "straight in de eye." In lieu of sexuality the movie-makers have dreamed up some mumbo jumbo involving buzzards' wings, signs of the zodiac, and death-dealing cards, so that, it appears, Carmen ruins Joe because she loves him and decides to leave him because the cards tell her she is going to die. The fact that between the time she leaves him and the time he kills her she acquires some new clothes, and drinks — as one of her arias rather violently indicates she intends to — a great deal of champagne is simply a sign of her intense inner suffering.

Carmen has come a long way from the auction block, but Joe, of course, cannot be far behind. This Joe is a good, fine-looking boy who loves his Maw, has studied hard, and is going to be sent to flying school, and who is engaged to a girl who rather resembles his Maw, named Cindy Lou. His indifference to Carmen, who has all the other males in sight quivering with a passion never seen on land or sea, sets her ablaze; in a series of scenes which it is difficult to call erotic without adding that they are also infantile, she goes after him and he falls. Here the technicolored bodies of Dandridge and Belafonte, while the movie is being glum about the ruin of Joe's career and impending doom, are used for the maximum erotic effect. It is a sterile and distressing eroticism, however, because it is occurring in a vacuum between two mannequins who clearly are not involved in anything more serious than giving the customers a run for their money. One is not watching either tenderness or love, and one is certainly not watching the complex and consuming passion which leads to life or death — one is watching a timorous and vulgar misrepresentation of these things.

And it must be said that one of the reasons for this is that, while the movie-makers are pleased to have Miss Dandridge flouncing about in tight skirts and plunging necklines — which is not exactly sexuality, either — the Negro male is still too loaded a quantity for them to know quite how to handle. The result is that Mr. Belafonte is really not allowed to do anything more than walk around looking like a spaniel: *his* sexuality is really taken as given because Miss Dandridge wants him. It does not, otherwise, exist and he is not destroyed by his own sexual aggressiveness, which he is not allowed to have, but by the sexual aggressiveness of the girl — or, as it turns out, not even really by that, but by tea leaves. The only reason, finally, that the eroticism of *Carmen Jones* is more potent than, say, the eroticism of a Lana Turner vehicle is that *Carmen Jones* has Negro bodies before the camera and Negroes are associated in the public mind with sex. Since darker races always seem to have for lighter races an aura of sexuality, this fact is not distressing in itself. What is distressing is the conjecture this movie leaves one with as to what Americans take sex to be.

The most important thing about this movie — and the reason that, despite itself, it is one of the most important all-Negro movies Hollywood has yet produced — is that the questions it leaves in the mind relate less to Negroes than to the interior life of Americans. One wonders, it is true, if Negroes are really going to become the ciphers this movie makes them out to be; but, since they have until now survived public images even more appalling, one is encouraged to hope, for their sake and the sake of the Republic, that they will continue to prove themselves incorrigible. Besides, life does not produce ciphers like these: when people have become this empty they are not ciphers any longer, but monsters. The creation of such ciphers proves, however, that Americans are far from empty; they are, on the contrary, very deeply disturbed. And this disturbance is not the kind which can be eased by the doing of good works, but seems to have turned inward and shows every sign of becoming personal. This is one of the best things that can possibly happen. It can be taken to mean — among a great many other things — that the ferment which has resulted in as odd a brew as *Carmen Jones* can now be expected to produce something which will be more bitter on the tongue but sweeter in the stomach.

PART TWO

The Harlem Ghetto

Harlem, physically at least, has changed very little in my parents' lifetime or in mine. Now as then the buildings are old and in desperate need of repair, the streets are crowded and dirty, there are too many human beings per square block. Rents are 10 to 58 per cent higher than anywhere else in the city; food, expensive everywhere, is more expensive here and of an inferior quality; and now that the war is over and money is dwindling, clothes are carefully shopped for and seldom bought. Negroes, traditionally the last to be hired and the first to be fired, are finding jobs harder to get, and, while prices are rising implacably, wages are going down. All over Harlem now there is felt the same bitter expectancy with which, in my childhood, we awaited winter: it is coming and it will be hard; there is nothing anyone can do about it.

All of Harlem is pervaded by a sense of congestion, rather like the insistent, maddening, claustrophobic pounding in the skull that comes from trying to breathe in a very small room with all the windows shut. Yet the white man walking through Harlem is not at all likely to find it sinister or more wretched than any other slum.

Harlem wears to the casual observer a casual face; no one remarks that — considering the history of black men and women and the legends that have sprung up about them, to say nothing of the ever-present policemen, wary on the street corners — the face is, indeed, somewhat excessively casual and may not be as open or as careless as it seems. If an outbreak of more than usual violence occurs, as in 1935 or in 1943, it is met with sorrow and surprise and rage; the social hostility of the rest of the city feeds on this as proof that they were right all along, and the hostility increases; speeches are made, committees are set up, investigations ensue. Steps are taken to right the wrong, without, however, expanding or demolishing the ghetto. The idea is to make it less of a social liability, a process about as helpful as make-up to a leper. Thus, we have the Boys' Club on West 134th Street, the playground at West 131st and Fifth Avenue; and, since Negroes will not be allowed to live in Stuyvesant Town, Metropolitan Life is thoughtfully erecting a housing project called Riverton in the center of Harlem; however, it is not likely that any but the professional class of Negroes — and not all of them — will be able to pay the rent.

Most of these projects have been stimulated by perpetually embattled Negro leaders and by the Negro press. Concerning Negro leaders, the best that one can say is that they are in an impossible position and that the handful motivated by genuine concern maintain this position with heartbreaking dignity. It is unlikely that anyone acquainted with Harlem seriously assumes that the presence of one playground more or less has any profound effect upon the psychology of the citizens there. And yet it is better to have the playground; it is better than nothing; and it will, at least, make life somewhat easier for parents who will then know that their children are not in as much danger of being run down in the streets. Similarly, even though the American cult of literacy has chiefly operated only to provide a market for the *Reader's Digest* and the *Daily News*, literacy is still better than illiteracy; so Negro leaders must demand more and better schools for Negroes, though any Negro who takes this schooling at face value will find himself virtually incapacitated for life in this democracy. Possibly the most salutary effect of all this activity is that it assures the Negro that he is not altogether forgotten: people *are* working in his behalf, however hopeless or misguided they may be; and as long as the water is troubled it cannot become stagnant.

The terrible thing about being a Negro leader lies in the term itself. I do not mean merely the somewhat condescending differentiation the term implies, but the nicely refined torture a man can experience from having been created and defeated by the same circumstances. That is, Negro leaders have been created by the American scene, which thereafter works against them at every point; and the best that they can hope for is ultimately to work themselves out of their jobs, to nag contemporary American leaders and the members of their own group until a bad situation becomes so complicated and so bad that it cannot be endured any longer. It is like needling a blister until it bursts. On the other hand, one cannot help observing that some Negro leaders and politicians are far more concerned with their careers than with the welfare of Negroes, and their dramatic and publicized battles are battles with the wind. Again, this phenomenon cannot be changed without a change in the American scene. In a land where, it is said, any citizen can grow up and become president, Negroes can be pardoned for desiring to enter Congress.

The Negro press, which supports any man, provided he is sufficiently dark and well-known — with the exception of certain Negro novelists accused of drawing portraits unflattering to the race — has for years received vastly confusing criticism based on the fact that it is helplessly and always exactly what it calls itself, that is, a press devoted entirely to happenings in or about the Negro world. This preoccupation can probably be forgiven in view of the great indifference and frequent hostility of the American white press. The Negro press has been accused of not helping matters much — as indeed, it has not, nor do I see how it could have. And it has been accused of being sensational, which it is; but this is a criticism difficult to take seriously in a country so devoted to the sensational as ours.

The best-selling Negro newspaper, I believe, is the *Amsterdam Star-News*, which is also the worst, being gleefully devoted to murders, rapes, raids on love-nests, interracial wars, any item — however meaningless — concerning prominent Negroes, and whatever racial gains can be reported for the week — all in just about that order. Apparently, this policy works well; it sells papers — which is, after all, the aim; in my childhood we never missed an edition. The day the paper came out we could hear, far down the street, the news vendor screaming the latest scandal and people rushing to read about it.

The *Amsterdam* has been rivaled, in recent years, by the *People's Voice*, a journal, modeled on *PM* and referred to as *PV*. *PV* is not so wildly sensational a paper as the *Amsterdam*, though its coverage is much the same (the news coverage of the Negro press is naturally pretty limited). *PV*'s politics are less murky, to the left of center

THE HARLEM GHETTO

61

(the *Amsterdam* is Republican, a political affiliation that
has led it into some strange doubletalk), and its tone, since
its inception, has been ever more hopelessly militant, full
of warnings, appeals, and open letters to the government
— which, to no one's surprise, are not answered — and
the same rather pathetic preoccupation with prominent
Negroes and what they are doing. Columns signed by
Lena Horne and Paul Robeson appeared in *PV* until several weeks ago, when both severed their connections with
the paper. Miss Horne's column made her sound like an
embittered Eleanor Roosevelt, and the only column of
Robeson's I have read was concerned with the current
witch-hunt in Hollywood, discussing the kind of movies
under attack and Hollywood's traditional treatment of
Negroes. It is personally painful to me to realize that so
gifted and forceful a man as Robeson should have been
tricked by his own bitterness and by a total inability to
understand the nature of political power in general, or
Communist aims in particular, into missing the point of
his own critique, which is worth a great deal of thought:
that there are a great many ways of being un-American,
some of them nearly as old as the country itself, and that
the House Un-American Activities Committee might find
concepts and attitudes even more damaging to American
life in a picture like *Gone With the Wind* than in the
possibly equally romantic but far less successful *Watch
on the Rhine.*

The only other newspapers in the field with any significant sale in Harlem are the Pittsburgh *Courier*, which
has the reputation of being the best of the lot, and the
Afro-American, which resembles the New York *Journal-
American* in layout and type and seems to make a con-

sistent if unsuccessful effort to be at once readable, intelligent, and fiery. The *Courier* is a high-class paper, reaching its peak in the handling of its society news and in the columns of George S. Schuyler, whose Olympian serenity infuriates me, but who, as a matter of fact, reflects with great accuracy the state of mind and the ambitions of the professional, well-to-do Negro who has managed to find a place to stand. Mr. Schuyler, who is remembered still for a satirical novel I have not read, called *Black No More,* is aided enormously in this position by a genteel white wife and a child-prodigy daughter — who is seriously regarded in some circles as proof of the incomprehensible contention that the mating of white and black is more likely to produce genius than any other combination. (The *Afro-American* recently ran a series of articles on this subject, "The Education of a Genius," by Mrs. Amarintha Work, who recorded in detail the development of her mulatto son, Craig.)

Ebony and *Our World* are the two big magazines in the field, *Ebony* looking and sounding very much like *Life,* and *Our World* being the black man's *Look. Our World* is a very strange, disorganized magazine indeed, sounding sometimes like a college newspaper and sometimes like a call to arms, but principally, like its more skillful brothers, devoted to the proposition that anything a white man can do a Negro can probably do better. *Ebony* digs feature articles out of such things as the "real" Lena Horne and Negro FBI agents, and it travels into the far corners of the earth for any news, however trivial, concerning any Negro or group of Negroes who are in any way unusual and/or newsworthy. The tone of both *Ebony* and *Our World* is affirmative; they cater to the "better class of Negro." *Ebony's* November 1947 issue carried an editoral entitled "Time To Count Our Blessings," which began by accusing Chester Himes (author of the novel *Lonely Crusade*) of having a color psychosis, and went on to explain that there are Negro racists also who are just as blind and dangerous as Bilbo, which is incontestably true, and that, compared to the millions of starving Europeans, Negroes are sitting pretty — which comparison, I hazard, cannot possibly mean anything to any Negro who has not seen Europe. The editorial concluded that Negroes had come a long way and that "as patriotic Americans" it was time "we" stopped singing the blues and realized just how bright the future was. These cheering sentiments were flanked — or underscored, if you will — by a photograph on the opposite page of an aging Negro farm woman carrying home a bumper crop of onions. It apparently escaped the editors of *Ebony* that the very existence of their magazine, and its table of contents for any month, gave the lie to this effort to make the best of a bad bargain.

The true *raison d'être* of the Negro press can be found in the letters-to-the-editor sections, where the truth about life among the rejected can be seen in print. It is the terrible dilemma of the Negro press that, having no other model, it models itself on the white press, attempting to emulate the same effortless, sophisticated tone — a tone its subject matter renders utterly unconvincing. It is simply impossible not to sing the blues, audibly or not, when the lives lived by Negroes are so inescapably harsh and stunted. It is not the Negro press that is at fault: whatever contradictions, inanities, and political infantilism can be charged to it can be charged equally to the American press at large. It is a black man's newspaper straining for recognition and a foothold in the white man's world. Matters are not helped in the least by the fact that the white man's world, intellectually, morally, and spiritually, has the meaningless ring of a hollow drum and the odor of slow death. Within the body of the Negro press all the wars and falsehoods, all the decay and dislocation and struggle of our society are seen in relief.

The Negro press, like the Negro, becomes the scapegoat for our ills. There is no difference, after all, between the *Amsterdam*'s handling of a murder on Lenox Avenue and the *Daily News'* coverage of a murder on Beekman Hill; nor is there any difference between the chauvinism of the two papers, except that the *News* is smug and the *Amsterdam* is desperate. Negroes live violent lives, unavoidably; a Negro press without violence is therefore not possible; and, further, in every act of violence, particularly violence against white men, Negroes feel a certain thrill of identification, a wish to have done it themselves, a feeling that old scores are being settled at last. It is no accident that Joe Louis is the most idolized man in Harlem. He has succeeded on a level that white America indicates is the only level for which it has any respect. We (Americans in general, that is) like to point to Negroes and to most of their activities with a kind of tolerant scorn; but it is ourselves we are watching, ourselves we are damning, or — condescendingly — bending to save.

I have written at perhaps excessive length about the Negro press, principally because its many critics have always seemed to me to make the irrational demand that the nation's most oppressed minority behave itself at all times with a skill and foresight no one ever expected of the late Joseph Patterson or ever expected of Hearst; and I have tried to give some idea of its tone because it seems to me that it is here that the innate desperation is betrayed. As for the question of Negro advertising, which has caused so much comment, it seems to me quite logical that any minority identified by the color of its skin and the texture of its hair would eventually grow self-conscious about these attributes and avoid advertising lotions that made the hair kinkier and soaps that darkened the skin. The American ideal, after all, is that everyone should be as much alike as possible.

It is axiomatic that the Negro is religious, which is to say that he stands in fear of the God our ancestors gave us and before whom we all tremble yet. There are probably more churches in Harlem than in any other ghetto in this city and they are going full blast every night and some of them are filled with praying people every day. This, supposedly, exemplifies the Negro's essential simplicity and good-will; but it is actually a fairly desperate emotional business.

These churches range from the august and publicized Abyssinian Baptist Church on West 138th Street to resolutely unclassifiable lofts, basements, store-fronts, and even private dwellings. Nightly, Holyroller ministers, spiritualists, self-appointed prophets and Messiahs gather their flocks together for worship and for strength through joy. And this is not, as *Cabin in the Sky* would have us believe, merely a childlike emotional release. Their faith may be described as childlike, but the end it serves is often sinister. It may, indeed, "keep them happy" — a phrase carrying the inescapable inference that the way of life imposed on Negroes makes them quite actively unhappy

— but also, and much more significantly, religion operates here as a complete and exquisite fantasy revenge: white people own the earth and commit all manner of abomination and injustice on it; the bad will be punished and the good rewarded, for God is not sleeping, the judgment is not far off. It does not require a spectacular degree of perception to realize that bitterness is here neither dead nor sleeping, and that the white man, believing what he wishes to believe, has misread the symbols. Quite often the Negro preacher descends to levels less abstract and leaves no doubt as to what is on his mind: the pressure of life in Harlem, the conduct of the Italian-Ethiopian war, racial injustice during the recent war, and the terrible possibility of yet another very soon. All these topics provide excellent springboards for sermons thinly coated with spirituality but designed mainly to illustrate the injustice of the white American and anticipate his certain and long overdue punishment.

Here, too, can be seen one aspect of the Negro's ambivalent relation to the Jew. To begin with, though the traditional Christian accusation that the Jews killed Christ is neither questioned nor doubted, the term "Jew" actually operates in this initial context to include all infidels of white skin who have failed to accept the Savior. No real distinction is made: the preacher begins by accusing the Jews of having refused the light and proceeds from there to a catalog of their subsequent sins and the sufferings visited on them by a wrathful God. Though the notion of the suffering is based on the image of the wandering, exiled Jew, the context changes imperceptibly, to become a fairly obvious reminder of the trials of the Negro, while the sins recounted are the sins of the American republic.

At this point, the Negro identifies himself almost wholly with the Jew. The more devout Negro considers that he *is* a Jew, in bondage to a hard taskmaster and waiting for a Moses to lead him out of Egypt. The hymns, the texts, and the most favored legends of the devout Negro are all Old Testament and therefore Jewish in origin: the flight from Egypt, the Hebrew children in the fiery furnace, the terrible jubilee songs of deliverance: *Lord, wasn't that hard trials, great tribulations, I'm bound to leave this land!* The covenant God made in the beginning with Abraham and which was to extend to his children and to his children's children forever is a covenant made with these latter-day exiles also: as Israel was chosen, so are they. The birth and death of Jesus, which adds a non-Judaic element, also implements this identification. It is the covenant made with Abraham again, renewed, signed with his blood. ("Before Abraham was, I am.") Here the figure of Jesus operates as the intercessor, the bridge from earth to heaven; it was Jesus who made it possible, who made salvation free to all, "to the Jew first and afterwards the Gentile." The images of the suffering Christ and the suffering Jew are wedded with the image of the suffering slave, and they are one: the people that walked in darkness have seen a great light.

But if the Negro has bought his salvation with pain and the New Testament is used to prove, as it were, the validity of the transformation, it is the Old Testament which is clung to and most frequently preached from, which provides the emotional fire and anatomizes the path of bondage; and which promises vengeance and assures the chosen of their place in Zion. The favorite text of my father, among the most earnest of ministers, was not

"Father, forgive them, for they know not what they do," but "How can I sing the Lord's song in a strange land?" This same identification, which Negroes, since slavery, have accepted with their mothers' milk, serves, in contemporary actuality, to implement an involved and specific bitterness. Jews in Harlem are small tradesmen, rent collectors, real estate agents, and pawnbrokers; they operate in accordance with the American business tradition of exploiting Negroes, and they are therefore identified with oppression and are hated for it. I remember meeting no Negro in the years of my growing up, in my family or out of it, who would really ever trust a Jew, and few who did not, indeed, exhibit for them the blackest contempt. On the other hand, this did not prevent their working for Jews, being utterly civil and pleasant to them, and, in most cases, contriving to delude their employers into believing that, far from harboring any dislike for Jews, they would rather work for a Jew than for anyone else. It is part of the price the Negro pays for his position in this society that, as Richard Wright points out, he is almost always acting. A Negro learns to gauge precisely what reaction the alien person facing him desires, and he produces it with disarming artlessness. The friends I had, growing up and going to work, grew more bitter every day; and, conversely, they learned to hide this bitterness and to fit into the pattern Gentile and Jew alike had fixed for them.

The tension between Negroes and Jews contains an element not characteristic of Negro-Gentile tension, an element which accounts in some measure for the Negro's tendency to castigate the Jew verbally more often than the Gentile, and which might lead one to the conclusion

that, of all white people on the face of the earth, it is the
Jew whom the Negro hates most. When the Negro hates
the Jew *as a Jew* he does so partly because the nation
does and in much the same painful fashion that he hates
himself. It is an aspect of his humiliation whittled down
to a manageable size and then transferred; it is the best
form the Negro has for tabulating vocally his long record
of grievances against his native land.

At the same time, there is a subterranean assumption
that the Jew should "know better," that he has suffered
enough himself to know what suffering means. An understanding is expected of the Jew such as none but the most
naïve and visionary Negro has ever expected of the American Gentile. The Jew, by the nature of his own precarious
position, has failed to vindicate this faith. Jews, like
Negroes, must use every possible weapon in order to be
accepted, and must try to cover their vulnerability by a
frenzied adoption of the customs of the country; and the
nation's treatment of Negroes is unquestionably a custom.
The Jew has been taught — and, too often, accepts — the
legend of Negro inferiority; and the Negro, on the other
hand, has found nothing in his experience with Jews to
counteract the legend of Semitic greed. Here the American white Gentile has two legends serving him at once:
he has divided these minorities and he rules.

It seems unlikely that within this complicated structure
any real and systematic cooperation can be achieved between Negroes and Jews. (This is in terms of the over-all
social problem and is not meant to imply that individual
friendships are impossible or that they are valueless when
they occur.) The structure of the American commonwealth has trapped both these minorities into attitudes

of perpetual hostility. They do not dare trust each other — the Jew because he feels he must climb higher on the American social ladder and has, so far as he is concerned, nothing to gain from identification with any minority even more unloved than he; while the Negro is in the even less tenable position of not really daring to trust anyone.

This applies, with qualifications and yet with almost no exceptions, even to those Negroes called progressive and "unusual." Negroes of the professional class (as distinct from professional Negroes) compete actively with the Jew in daily contact; and they wear anti-Semitism as a defiant proof of their citizenship; their positions are too shaky to allow them any real ease or any faith in anyone. They do not trust whites or each other or themselves; and, particularly and vocally, they do not trust Jews. During my brief days as a Socialist I spent more than one meeting arguing against anti-Semitism with a Negro college student, who was trying to get into civil service and was supporting herself meanwhile as a domestic. She was by no means a stupid girl, nor even a particularly narrow-minded one: she was all in favor of the millennium, even to working with Jews to achieve it; but she was not prepared ever to accept a Jew as a friend. It did no good to point out, as I did, that the exploitation of which she accused the Jews was American, not Jewish, that in fact, behind the Jewish face stood the American reality. And *my* Jewish friends in high school were not like that, I said, they had no intention of exploiting *me*, we did not hate each other. (I remember, as I spoke, being aware of doubt crawling like fog in the back of my mind.) This might all be very well, she told me, we were children now, with no need to earn a living. Wait until later, when your friends go into business and you try to get a job. You'll see!

It is this bitterness — felt alike by the inarticulate, hungry population of Harlem, by the wealthy on Sugar Hill, and by the brilliant exceptions ensconced in universities — which has defeated and promises to continue to defeat all efforts at interracial understanding. I am not one of the people who believe that oppression imbues a people with wisdom or insight or sweet charity, though the survival of the Negro in this country would simply not have been possible if this bitterness had been all he felt. In America, though, life seems to move faster than anywhere else on the globe and each generation is promised more than it will get: which creates, in each generation, a furious, bewildered rage, the rage of people who cannot find solid ground beneath their feet. Just as a mountain of sociological investigations, committee reports, and plans for recreational centers have failed to change the face of Harlem or prevent Negro boys and girls from growing up and facing, individually and alone, the unendurable frustration of being always, everywhere, inferior — until finally the cancer attacks the mind and warps it — so there seems no hope for better Negro-Jewish relations without a change in the American pattern.

Both the Negro and the Jew are helpless; the pressure of living is too immediate and incessant to allow time for understanding. I can conceive of no Negro native to this country who has not, by the age of puberty, been irreparably scarred by the conditions of his life. All over Harlem, Negro boys and girls are growing into stunted maturity, trying desperately to find a place to stand; and the wonder is not that so many are ruined but that so many survive.

The Negro's outlets are desperately constricted. In his dilemma he turns first upon himself and then upon whatever most represents to him his own emasculation. Here the Jew is caught in the American crossfire. The Negro, facing a Jew, hates, at bottom, not his Jewishness but the color of his skin. It is not the Jewish tradition by which he has been betrayed but the tradition of his native land. But just as a society must have a scapegoat, so hatred must have a symbol. Georgia has the Negro and Harlem has the Jew.

Journey to Atlanta

The Progressive Party has not, so far as I can gather, made any very great impression in Harlem, and this is not so much despite as because of its campaign promises, promises rather too extravagant to be believed. It is considered a rather cheerful axiom that all Americans distrust politicians. (No one takes the further and less cheerful step of considering just what effect this mutual contempt has on either the public or the politicians, who have, indeed, very little to do with one another.) Of all Americans, Negroes distrust politicians most, or, more accurately, they have been best trained to expect nothing from them; more than other Americans, they are always aware of the enormous gap between election promises and their daily lives. It is true that the promises excite them, but this is not because they are taken as proof of good intentions. They are the proof of something more concrete than intentions: that the Negro situation is not static, that changes have occurred, and are occurring and will occur — this, in spite of the daily, dead-end monotony. It is this daily, dead-end monotony, though, as well as the wise desire not to be betrayed by too much hoping, which causes them to look on politicians with such an extraordinarily disenchanted eye.

This fatalistic indifference is something that drives the

optimistic American liberal quite mad; he is prone, in his more exasperated moments, to refer to Negroes as political children, an appellation not entirely just. Negro liberals, being consulted, assure us that this is something that will disappear with "education," a vast, all-purpose term, conjuring up visions of sunlit housing projects, stacks of copybooks and a race of well-soaped, dark-skinned people who never slur their R's. Actually, this is not so much political irresponsibility as the product of experience, experience which no amount of education can quite efface. It is, as much as anything else, the reason the Negro vote is so easily bought and sold, the reason for that exclamation heard so frequently on Sugar Hill: "Our people never get anywhere."

"Our people" have functioned in this country for nearly a century as political weapons, the trump card up the enemies' sleeve; anything promised Negroes at election time is also a threat levelled at the opposition; in the struggle for mastery the Negro is the pawn. It is inescapable that this is only possible because of his position in this country and it has very frequently seemed at least equally apparent that this is a position which no one, least of all the politician, seriously intended to change.

Since Negroes have been in this country their one major, devastating gain was their Emancipation, an emancipation no one regards any more as having been dictated by humanitarian impulses. All that has followed from that brings to mind the rather unfortunate image of bones thrown to a pack of dogs sufficiently hungry to be dangerous. If all this sounds rather deliberately grim, it is not through any wish to make the picture darker than it is; I would merely like to complete the picture usually presented by pointing out that no matter how many instances there have been of genuine concern and good-will, nor how many hard, honest struggles have been carried on to improve the position of the Negro people, their position has not, in fact, changed so far as most of them are concerned.

Sociologists and historians, having the historical perspective in mind, may conclude that we are moving toward ever-greater democracy; but this is beyond the ken of a Negro growing up in any one of this country's ghettos. As regards Negro politicians, they are considered with pride as *politicians,* a pride much akin to that felt concerning Marian Anderson or Joe Louis: they have proven the worth of the Negro people and in terms, American terms, which no one can negate. But as no housewife expects Marian Anderson's genius to be of any practical aid in her dealings with the landlord, so nothing is expected of Negro representatives. The terrible thing, and here we have an American phenomenon in relief, is the fact that the Negro representative, by virtue of his position, is ever more removed from the people he ostensibly serves. Moreover, irrespective of personal integrity, his position — neatly and often painfully paradoxical — is utterly dependent on the continuing debasement of fourteen million Negroes; should the national ideals be put into practice tomorrow, countless prominent Negroes would lose their *raison d'être.*

Finally, we are confronted with the psychology and tradition of the country; if the Negro vote is so easily bought and sold, it is because it has been treated with so little respect; since no Negro dares seriously assume that any politician is concerned with the fate of Negroes, or would do much about it if he had the power, the vote must be bartered for what it will get, for whatever short-term goals can be managed. These goals are mainly economic and frequently personal, sometimes pathetic: bread or a new roof or five dollars, or, continuing up the scale, schools, houses or more Negroes in hitherto Caucasian jobs. The American commonwealth chooses to overlook what Negroes are never able to forget: they are not *really* considered a part of it. Like Aziz in *A Passage to India* or Topsy in *Uncle Tom's Cabin,* they know that white people, whatever their love for justice, have no love for them.

This is the crux of the matter; and the Progressive Party, with its extravagant claims, has, therefore, imposed on itself the considerable burden of proof. The only party within recent memory which made equally strident claims of fellowship were the Communists, who failed to survive this test; and the only politician of similar claims was, of course, Wallace's erstwhile master, Roosevelt, who did not after all, now that the magic of his voice is gone, succeed in raising the darker brother to the status of a citizen. This is the ancestry of the Wallace party, and it does not work wholly in its favor. It operates to give pause to even the most desperate and the most gullible.

It is, however, considered on one level, the level of short-term goals, with approval, since it does afford temporary work for Negroes, particularly those associated in any manner with the arts. The rather flippant question on 125th Street now is: "So? You working for Mr. Wallace these days?" For at least there is that: entertainers, personalities are in demand. To forestall lawsuits, I must explain that I am not discussing "names" — who are in rather a different position, too touchy and complex to analyze here — but the unknown, the struggling, endless armies of Negro boys and girls bent on, and as yet very far from, recognition. A segment of this army, a quartet called *The Melodeers,* made a trip to Atlanta under the auspices of the Progressive Party in August, a trip which lasted about eighteen days and which left them with no love for Mr. Wallace. Since this quartet included two of my brothers, I was given the details of the trip; indeed, David, the younger, kept a sort of journal for me — literally a blow-by-blow account.

Harlem is filled with churches and on Sundays it gives the impression of being filled with music. Quartets such as my brothers' travel from church to church in the fashion of circuit preachers, singing as much for the love of singing and the need for practice as for the rather indifferent sums collected for them which are then divided. These quartets have "battles of song," the winning team adding, of course, immensely to its prestige, the most consistent winners being the giants in this field. The aim of all these quartets, of course, is to branch out, to hit the big time and sing for a livelihood. The Golden Gate Quartet, judging at least from its music, had its roots here, and out of such a background came Sister Rosetta Tharpe, whom I heard, not quite ten years ago, plunking a guitar in a storefront church on Fifth Avenue. *The Melodeers* have not been singing very long and are very far from well-known, and the invitation to sing on tour with the Wallace party in the South seemed, whatever their misgivings about the Mason-Dixon line, too good an opportunity to pass up.

This invitation, by the way, seems to have been the brainstorm of a Clarence Warde, a Negro merchant seaman once employed as a cottage father in a corrective institution up-state; it was he in New York who acted as a go-between, arranging, since *The Melodeers* are minors, to be their legal guardian and manager on the road. An extended tour, such as was planned, met with some opposition from the parents, an opposition countered by the possible long-term benefits of the tour in so far as the boys' careers were concerned and, even more urgently, by the assurance that, at the very least, the boys would come home with a considerably larger sum of money than any of them were making on their jobs. (The political implications do not seem to have carried much weight.) A series of churches had been lined up for them presumably throughout the South. "The understanding," writes David, "was that we were supposed to sing"; after which the party was to take over to make speeches and circulate petitions. "The arrangement," David notes laconically, "sounded very promising, so we decided to go."

And, indeed, they traveled South in splendor, in a Pullman, to be exact, in which, since what David describes as a "Southern gentleman and wife" took exception to their presence, they traveled alone.

At the Wallace headquarters in Atlanta they were introduced to a Mrs. Branson Price, a grey-haired white woman of incurably aristocratic leanings who seems to have been the directress of the party in that region. The graciousness of her reception was only slightly marred by the fact that she was not expecting singers and thought they were a new group of canvassers. She arranged for them to take rooms on Butler Street at the YMCA. Here the first gap between promise and performance was made manifest, a gap, they felt, which was perhaps too trifling to make a fuss about. In New York they had been promised comparative privacy, two to a room; but now, it developed, they were to sleep in a dormitory. This gap, in fact, it was the province of Mr. Warde to close, but whether he was simply weary from the trip or overwhelmed by the aristocratic Mrs. Price, he kept his mouth shut and, indeed, did not open it again for quite some time.

When they returned to headquarters, somewhat irritated at having had to wait three hours for the arrival of Louis Burner, who had the money for their rooms, Mrs. Price suggested that they go out canvassing. This was wholly unexpected, since no one had mentioned canvassing in New York and, since, moreover, canvassers are voluntary workers who are not paid. Further, the oldest of them was twenty, which was not voting age, and none of them knew anything about the Progressive Party, nor did they care much. On the other hand, it is somewhat difficult to refuse a grey-haired, aristocratic lady who is toiling day and night for the benefit of your people; and Mr. Warde, who should have been their spokesman, had not yet recovered his voice; so they took the petitions, which were meant to put the Wallace party on the ballot, and began knocking on doors in the Negro section of Atlanta. They were sent out in pairs, white and black, a political device which operates not only as the living proof of brotherhood, but which has the additional virtue of intimidating into passive silence the more susceptible beholder, who cannot, after all, unleash the impatient scorn he may feel with a strange, benevolent white man sitting in his parlor.

They canvassed for three days, during which time their expenses — $2.25 per man per day — were paid, but during which time they were doing no singing and making no money. On the third day they pointed out that this was not quite what they had been promised in New York, to be met with another suggestion from the invincible Mrs. Price: how would they like to sing on the sound-truck? They had not the faintest desire to sing on a sound-truck, especially when they had been promised a string of churches; however, the churches, along with Mr. Warde's vigor, seemed unavailable at the moment; they could hardly sit around Atlanta doing nothing; and so long as they worked with the party they were certain, at least, to be fed. "The purpose of our singing," David writes, "was to draw a crowd so the party could make speeches." Near the end of the singing and during the speeches, leaflets and petitions were circulated through the crowd.

David had not found Negroes in the South different in any important respect from Negroes in the North; except that many of them were distrustful and "they are always talking about the North; they have to let you know they know somebody in New York or Chicago or Detroit." Of the crowds that gathered — and, apparently, *The Melodeers* attracted great numbers — "many of these people couldn't read or write their names" and not many of them knew anything at all about the Progressive Party. But they did divine, as American Negroes must, what was expected of them; and they listened to the speeches and signed the petitions.

Becoming both desperate and impatient, *The Melodeers* began making engagements and singing on their own, stealing time from canvassing to rehearse. They made more appointments than they were able to keep; partly because the lack of money limited their mobility but also because the Party, discovering these clandestine appointments, moved in, demanding to be heard. Those churches which refused to make room for the Party were not allowed to hear the quartet, which thus lost its last hope of making any money. The quartet wondered what had happened to Mr. Warde. David's account all but ignores him until nearly the end of the trip, when his position during all this is perhaps given some illumination.

Things now began to go steadily worse. They got into an argument with the manager of the Y, who objected to their rehearsing, and moved to a private home, for which the Party paid 75¢ per man per day; and the Party, which was, one gathers, furiously retrenching, arranged for them to eat at Fraziers' Cafe, a Negro establishment on Hunter Street, for $1.25 per man per day. My correspondent notes that they had no choice of meals — "they served us what they liked" — which seems to have been mainly limp vegetables — and "we were as hungry when we walked out as we were when we walked in." On the other hand, they were allowed to choose their beverage: tea or coffee or soda pop.

Heaven only knows what prompted Mrs. Branson Price to give a party at this point. Perhaps the campaign was going extraordinarily well; perhaps Fraziers' Cafe, where the party was held, was in need of a little extra revenue as well as the knowledge that its adoption of the Party would help to bring about a better world; perhaps Mrs. Price merely longed to be a gracious hostess once again. In any case, on a Sunday night she gave a party to which everyone was invited. My brother, who at this point was much concerned with food, observed glumly, "We had ice-cream."

The quartet sat at a table by itself, robbed, however, of the presence of Mr. Warde, who was invited to sit at Mrs. Price's table: "she said it would be an honor," my correspondent notes, failing, however, to say for whom. "There was a man there called a *folk*-singer," says David with venom, "and, naturally, everybody had to hear some *folk* songs." Eventually, the folksy aspect of the evening was exhausted and the quartet was invited to sing. They sang four selections, apparently to everyone's delight for they had to be quite adamant about not singing a fifth. The strain of continual singing in the open air had done their voices no good and it had made one of them extremely hoarse. So they refused, over loud protests, and apologized. "This displeased Mrs. Price."

Indeed, it had. She was not in the least accustomed to having her suggestions, to say nothing of her requests, refused. Early Monday morning she called Mr. Warde to her office to inquire who those black boys thought they were? and determined to ship them all back that same day in a car. Mr. Warde, who, considering the honors of the evening before, must have been rather astounded, protested such treatment, to be warned that she might very well ship them off without a car; the six of them might very well be forced to take to the road. This is not a pleasant mode of traveling for a Negro in the North and no Negro in Atlanta, particularly no Northern Negro, is likely to get very far. Mr. Warde temporized: they could not leave on such short notice; for one thing, the boys had clothes at the cleaners which would not be ready for a while and which they could hardly afford to lose. Mrs.

Price, every aristocratic vein pounding, did not wish to be concerned with such plebeian matters and, finally, losing all patience, commanded Mr. Warde to leave her office: Had he forgotten that he was in Georgia? Didn't he know better than sit in a white woman's office?

Mr. Warde, in whose bowels last night's bread of fellowship must have acquired the weight of rock, left the office. Then the quartet attempted to secure an audience; to be met with implacable refusal and the threat of the police. There were, incidentally, according to my brother, five Negro policemen in Atlanta at this time, who, though they were not allowed to arrest whites, would, of course, be willing, indeed, in their position, anxious, to arrest any Negro who seemed to need it. In Harlem, Negro policemen are feared even more than whites, for they have more to prove and fewer ways to prove it. The prospect of being arrested in Atlanta made them a little dizzy with terror: what might mean a beating in Harlem might quite possibly mean death here. "And at the same time," David says, "it was funny"; by which he means that the five policemen were faint prophecies of that equality which is the Progressive Party's goal.

They did not see Mrs. Price again; this was their severance from the Party, which now refused to pay any expenses; it was only the fact that their rent had been paid in advance which kept them off the streets. Food, however, remained a problem. Mr. Warde brought them a "couple of loaves of bread" and some jam; they sang one engagement. During this week Mrs. Price relented enough to get their clothes from the cleaners and send Mr. Warde, in custody of a white man who had been at the party, to the bus station for tickets. This man, whose resemblance to the Southern Gentleman of the Pullman is in no way diminished by his allegiance to Mr. Wallace, bought the tickets and threw them on the ground at Mr. Warde's feet, advising him not to show his black face in Georgia again.

The quartet, meanwhile, had gotten together six dollars doing odd jobs, which was enough, perhaps, for three of them to eat on the road. They split up, three leaving that Friday and the other two staying on about ten days longer, working for a construction company. Mr. Warde stopped off to visit his family, promising to see *The Melodeers* in New York, but he had not arrived as this was being written. *The Melodeers* laugh about their trip now, that good-natured, hearty laughter which is, according to white men, the peculiar heritage of Negroes, Negroes who were born with the fortunate ability to laugh all their troubles away. Somewhat surprisingly, they are not particularly bitter toward the Progressive Party, though they can scarcely be numbered among its supporters. "They're all the same," David tells me, "ain't none of 'em gonna do you no good; if you gonna be foolish enough to believe what they say, then it serves you good and right. Ain't none of 'em gonna do a thing for *me*."

Notes of a Native Son

On the 29th of July, in 1943, my father died. On the same day, a few hours later, his last child was born. Over a month before this, while all our energies were concentrated in waiting for these events, there had been, in Detroit, one of the bloodiest race riots of the century. A few hours after my father's funeral, while he lay in state in the undertaker's chapel, a race riot broke out in Harlem. On the morning of the 3rd of August, we drove my father to the graveyard through a wilderness of smashed plate glass.

The day of my father's funeral had also been my nineteenth birthday. As we drove him to the graveyard, the spoils of injustice, anarchy, discontent, and hatred were all around us. It seemed to me that God himself had devised, to mark my father's end, the most sustained and brutally dissonant of codas. And it seemed to me, too, that the violence which rose all about us as my father left the world had been devised as a corrective for the pride of his eldest son. I had declined to believe in that apocalypse which had been central to my father's vision; very well, life seemed to be saying, here is something that will certainly pass for an apocalypse until the real thing comes along. I had inclined to be contemptuous of my father for the conditions of his life, for the conditions of our lives. When his life had ended I began to wonder about that life and also, in a new way, to be apprehensive about my own.

I had not known my father very well. We had got on badly, partly because we shared, in our different fashions, the vice of stubborn pride. When he was dead I realized that I had hardly ever spoken to him. When he had been dead a long time I began to wish I had. It seems to be typical of life in America, where opportunities, real and fancied, are thicker than anywhere else on the globe, that the second generation has no time to talk to the first. No one, including my father, seems to have known exactly how old he was, but his mother had been born during slavery. He was of the first generation of free men. He, along with thousands of other Negroes, came North after 1919 and I was part of that generation which had never seen the landscape of what Negroes sometimes call the Old Country.

He had been born in New Orleans and had been a quite young man there during the time that Louis Armstrong, a boy, was running errands for the dives and honky-tonks of what was always presented to me as one of the most wicked of cities — to this day, whenever I think of New Orleans, I also helplessly think of Sodom and Gomorrah. My father never mentioned Louis Armstrong, except to forbid us to play his records; but there was a picture of him on our wall for a long time. One of my father's strong-willed female relatives had placed it there and forbade my father to take it down. He never did, but he eventually maneuvered her out of the house and when, some

years later, she was in trouble and near death, he refused
to do anything to help her.

He was, I think, very handsome. I gather this from
photographs and from my own memories of him, dressed
in his Sunday best and on his way to preach a sermon
somewhere, when I was little. Handsome, proud, and
ingrown, "like a toe-nail," somebody said. But he looked
to me, as I grew older, like pictures I had seen of African
tribal chieftains: he really should have been naked, with
war-paint on and barbaric mementos, standing among
spears. He could be chilling in the pulpit and indescrib-
ably cruel in his personal life and he was certainly the
most bitter man I have ever met; yet it must be said that
there was something else in him, buried in him, which lent
him his tremendous power and, even, a rather crushing
charm. It had something to do with his blackness, I think
— he was very black — with his blackness and his beauty,
and with the fact that he knew that he was black but did
not know that he was beautiful. He claimed to be proud
of his blackness but it had also been the cause of much
humiliation and it had fixed bleak boundaries to his life.
He was not a young man when we were growing up and
he had already suffered many kinds of ruin; in his out-
rageously demanding and protective way he loved his
children, who were black like him and menaced, like
him; and all these things sometimes showed in his face
when he tried, never to my knowledge with any success,
to establish contact with any of us. When he took one of
his children on his knee to play, the child always became fretful and began to cry; when he tried to help
one of us with our homework the absolutely unabating

tension which emanated from him caused our minds and our tongues to become paralyzed, so that he, scarcely knowing why, flew into a rage and the child, not knowing why, was punished. If it ever entered his head to bring a surprise home for his children, it was, almost unfailingly, the wrong surprise and even the big watermelons he often brought home on his back in the summertime led to the most appalling scenes. I do not remember, in all those years, that one of his children was ever glad to see him come home. From what I was able to gather of his early life, it seemed that this inability to establish contact with other people had always marked him and had been one of the things which had driven him out of New Orleans. There was something in him, therefore, groping and tentative, which was never expressed and which was buried with him. One saw it most clearly when he was facing new people and hoping to impress them. But he never did, not for long. We went from church to smaller and more improbable church, he found himself in less and less demand as a minister, and by the time he died none of his friends had come to see him for a long time. He had lived and died in an intolerable bitterness of spirit and it frightened me, as we drove him to the graveyard through those unquiet, ruined streets, to see how powerful and overflowing this bitterness could be and to realize that this bitterness now was mine.

When he died I had been away from home for a little over a year. In that year I had had time to become aware of the meaning of all my father's bitter warnings, had discovered the secret of his proudly pursed lips and rigid carriage: I had discovered the weight of white people in the world. I saw that this had been for my ancestors and now would be for me an awful thing to live with and that the bitterness which had helped to kill my father could also kill me.

He had been ill a long time — in the mind, as we now realized, reliving instances of his fantastic intransigence in the new light of his affliction and endeavoring to feel a sorrow for him which never, quite, came true. We had not known that he was being eaten up by paranoia, and the discovery that his cruelty, to our bodies and our minds, had been one of the symptoms of his illness was not, then, enough to enable us to forgive him. The younger children felt, quite simply, relief that he would not be coming home anymore. My mother's observation that it was he, after all, who had kept them alive all these years meant nothing because the problems of keeping children alive are not real for children. The older children felt, with my father gone, that they could invite their friends to the house without fear that their friends would be insulted or, as had sometimes happened with me, being told that their friends were in league with the devil and intended to rob our family of everything we owned. (I didn't fail to wonder, and it made me hate him, what on earth we owned that anybody else would want.)

His illness was beyond all hope of healing before anyone realized that he was ill. He had always been so strange and had lived, like a prophet, in such unimaginably close communion with the Lord that his long silences which were punctuated by moans and hallelujahs and snatches of old songs while he sat at the living-room window never seemed odd to us. It was not until he refused to eat because, he said, his family was trying to poison him that my mother was forced to accept as a fact what had, until then, been only an unwilling suspicion. When he was committed, it was discovered that he had tuberculosis and, as it turned out, the disease of his mind allowed the disease of his body to destroy him. For the doctors could not force him to eat, either, and, though he was fed intravenously, it was clear from the beginning that there was no hope for him.

In my mind's eye I could see him, sitting at the window, locked up in his terrors; hating and fearing every living soul including his children who had betrayed him, too, by reaching towards the world which had despised him. There were nine of us. I began to wonder what it could have felt like for such a man to have had nine children whom he could barely feed. He used to make little jokes about our poverty, which never, of course, seemed very funny to us; they could not have seemed very funny to him, either, or else our all too feeble response to them would never have caused such rages. He spent great energy and achieved, to our chagrin, no small amount of success in keeping us away from the people who surrounded us, people who had all-night rent parties to which we listened when we should have been sleeping, people who cursed and drank and flashed razor blades on Lenox Avenue. He could not understand why, if they had so much energy to spare, they could not use it to make their lives better. He treated almost everybody on our block with a most uncharitable asperity and neither they, nor, of course, their children were slow to reciprocate.

The only white people who came to our house were welfare workers and bill collectors. It was almost always my mother who dealt with them, for my father's temper, which was at the mercy of his pride, was never to be trusted. It was clear that he felt their very presence in his home to be a violation: this was conveyed by his carriage, almost ludicrously stiff, and by his voice, harsh and vindictively polite. When I was around nine or ten I wrote a play which was directed by a young, white schoolteacher, a woman, who then took an interest in me, and gave me books to read and, in order to corroborate my theatrical bent, decided to take me to see what she somewhat tactlessly referred to as "real" plays. Theatergoing was forbidden in our house, but, with the really cruel intuitiveness of a child, I suspected that the color of this woman's skin would carry the day for me. When, at school, she suggested taking me to the theater, I did not, as I might have done if she had been a Negro, find a way of discouraging her, but agreed that she should pick me up at my house one evening. I then, very cleverly, left all the rest to my mother, who suggested to my father, as I knew she would, that it would not be very nice to let such a kind woman make the trip for nothing. Also, since it was a schoolteacher, I imagine that my mother countered the idea of sin with the idea of "education," which word, even with my father, carried a kind of bitter weight.

Before the teacher came my father took me aside to ask *why* she was coming, what *interest* she could possibly have in our house, in a boy like me. I said I didn't know but I, too, suggested that it had something to do with education. And I understood that my father was waiting for me to say something — I didn't quite know what; perhaps that I wanted his protection against this teacher and her "education." I said none of these things and the teacher came and we went out. It was clear, during the brief interview in our living room, that my father was

agreeing very much against his will and that he would
have refused permission if he had dared. The fact that
he did not dare caused me to despise him: I had no way
of knowing that he was facing in that living room a wholly
unprecedented and frightening situation.

Later, when my father had been laid off from his job,
this woman became very important to us. She was really
a very sweet and generous woman and went to a great
deal of trouble to be of help to us, particularly during
one awful winter. My mother called her by the highest
name she knew: she said she was a "christian." My father
could scarcely disagree but during the four or five years
of our relatively close association he never trusted her
and was always trying to surprise in her open, Midwestern
face the genuine, cunningly hidden, and hideous motiva-
tion. In later years, particularly when it began to be clear
that this "education" of mine was going to lead me to
perdition, he became more explicit and warned me that
my white friends in high school were not really my friends
and that I would see, when I was older, how white people
would do anything to keep a Negro down. Some of them
could be nice, he admitted, but none of them were to be
trusted and most of them were not even nice. The best
thing was to have as little to do with them as possible.
I did not feel this way and I was certain, in my innocence,
that I never would.

But the year which preceded my father's death had
made a great change in my life. I had been living in New
Jersey, working in defense plants, working and living
among southerners, white and black. I knew about the
south, of course, and about how southerners treated
Negroes and how they expected them to behave, but it

had never entered my mind that anyone would look at me and expect *me* to behave that way. I learned in New Jersey that to be a Negro meant, precisely, that one was never looked at but was simply at the mercy of the reflexes the color of one's skin caused in other people. I acted in New Jersey as I had always acted, that is as though I thought a great deal of myself — I had to *act* that way — with results that were, simply, unbelievable. I had scarcely arrived before I had earned the enmity, which was extraordinarily ingenious, of all my superiors and nearly all my co-workers. In the beginning, to make matters worse, I simply did not know what was happening. I did not know what I had done, and I shortly began to wonder what *anyone* could possibly do, to bring about such unanimous, active, and unbearably vocal hostility. I knew about jim-crow but I had never experienced it. I went to the same self-service restaurant three times and stood with all the Princeton boys before the counter, waiting for a hamburger and coffee; it was always an extraordinarily long time before anything was set before me; but it was not until the fourth visit that I learned that, in fact, nothing had ever been set before me: I had simply picked something up. Negroes were not served there, I was told, and they had been waiting for me to realize that I was always the only Negro present. Once I was told this, I determined to go there all the time. But now they were ready for me and, though some dreadful scenes were subsequently enacted in that restaurant, I never ate there again.

It was the same story all over New Jersey, in bars, bowling alleys, diners, places to live. I was always being forced to leave, silently, or with mutual imprecations. I very

shortly became notorious and children giggled behind
me when I passed and their elders whispered or shouted
— they really believed that I was mad. And it did begin
to work on my mind, of course; I began to be afraid to go
anywhere and to compensate for this I went places to
which I really should not have gone and where, God
knows, I had no desire to be. My reputation in town
naturally enhanced my reputation at work and my working day became one long series of acrobatics designed to
keep me out of trouble. I cannot say that these acrobatics
succeeded. It began to seem that the machinery of the
organization I worked for was turning over, day and
night, with but one aim: to eject me. I was fired once, and
contrived, with the aid of a friend from New York, to get
back on the payroll; was fired again, and bounced back
again. It took a while to fire me for the third time, but the
third time took. There were no loopholes anywhere.
There was not even any way of getting back inside the
gates.

That year in New Jersey lives in my mind as though it
were the year during which, having an unsuspected pre-
dilection for it, I first contracted some dread, chronic
disease, the unfailing symptom of which is a kind of blind
fever, a pounding in the skull and fire in the bowels. Once
this disease is contracted, one can never be really carefree
again, for the fever, without an instant's warning, can
recur at any moment. It can wreck more important things
than race relations. There is not a Negro alive who does
not have this rage in his blood — one has the choice,
merely, of living with it consciously or surrendering to it.
As for me, this fever has recurred in me, and does, and
will until the day I die.

My last night in New Jersey, a white friend from New York took me to the nearest big town, Trenton, to go to the movies and have a few drinks. As it turned out, he also saved me from, at the very least, a violent whipping. Almost every detail of that night stands out very clearly in my memory. I even remember the name of the movie we saw because its title impressed me as being so patly ironical. It was a movie about the German occupation of France, starring Maureen O'Hara and Charles Laughton and called *This Land Is Mine*. I remember the name of the diner we walked into when the movie ended: it was the "American Diner." When we walked in the counterman asked what we wanted and I remember answering with the casual sharpness which had become my habit: "We want a hamburger and a cup of coffee, what do you think we want?" I do not know why, after a year of such rebuffs, I so completely failed to anticipate his answer, which was, of course, "We don't serve Negroes here." This reply failed to discompose me, at least for the moment. I made some sardonic comment about the name of the diner and we walked out into the streets.

This was the time of what was called the "brown-out," when the lights in all American cities were very dim. When we re-entered the streets something happened to me which had the force of an optical illusion, or a nightmare. The streets were very crowded and I was facing north. People were moving in every direction but it seemed to me, in that instant, that all of the people I could see, and many more than that, were moving toward me, against me, and that everyone was white. I remember how their faces gleamed. And I felt, like a physical sensation, a *click* at the nape of my neck as though some interior string connecting my head to my body had been cut. I began to walk. I heard my friend call after me, but I ignored him. Heaven only knows what was going on in his mind, but he had the good sense not to touch me — I don't know what would have happened if he had — and to keep me in sight. I don't know what was going on in my mind, either; I certainly had no conscious plan. I wanted to do something to crush these white faces, which were crushing me. I walked for perhaps a block or two until I came to an enormous, glittering, and fashionable restaurant in which I knew not even the intercession of the Virgin would cause me to be served. I pushed through the doors and took the first vacant seat I saw, at a table for two, and waited.

I do not know how long I waited and I rather wonder, until today, what I could possibly have looked like. Whatever I looked like, I frightened the waitress who shortly appeared, and the moment she appeared all of my fury flowed towards her. I hated her for her white face, and for her great, astounded, frightened eyes. I felt that if she found a black man so frightening I would make her fright worth-while.

She did not ask me what I wanted, but repeated, as though she had learned it somewhere, "We don't serve Negroes here." She did not say it with the blunt, derisive hostility to which I had grown so accustomed, but, rather, with a note of apology in her voice, and fear. This made me colder and more murderous than ever. I felt I had to do something with my hands. I wanted her to come close enough for me to get her neck between my hands.

So I pretended not to have understood her, hoping to draw her closer. And she did step a very short step closer, with her pencil poised incongruously over her pad, and repeated the formula: ". . . don't serve Negroes here."

Somehow, with the repetition of that phrase, which was already ringing in my head like a thousand bells of a nightmare, I realized that she would never come any closer and that I would have to strike from a distance. There was nothing on the table but an ordinary water-mug half full of water, and I picked this up and hurled it with all my strength at her. She ducked and it missed her and shattered against the mirror behind the bar. And, with that sound, my frozen blood abruptly thawed, I returned from wherever I had been, I *saw*, for the first time, the restaurant, the people with their mouths open, already, as it seemed to me, rising as one man, and I realized what I had done, and where I was, and I was frightened. I rose and began running for the door. A round, potbellied man grabbed me by the nape of the neck just as I reached the doors and began to beat me about the face. I kicked him and got loose and ran into the streets. My friend whispered, *"Run!"* and I ran.

My friend stayed outside the restaurant long enough to misdirect my pursuers and the police, who arrived, he told me, at once. I do not know what I said to him when he came to my room that night. I could not have said much. I felt, in the oddest, most awful way, that I had somehow betrayed him. I lived it over and over and over again, the way one relives an automobile accident after it has happened and one finds oneself alone and safe. I could not get over two facts, both equally difficult for the imagination to grasp, and one was that I could have been murdered. But the other was that I had been ready to commit murder. I saw nothing very clearly but I did

see this: that my life, my *real* life, was in danger, and not
from anything other people might do but from the hatred
I carried in my own heart.

II

I had returned home around the second week in June
— in great haste because it seemed that my father's death
and my mother's confinement were both but a matter of
hours. In the case of my mother, it soon became clear
that she had simply made a miscalculation. This had
always been her tendency and I don't believe that a single
one of us arrived in the world, or has since arrived anywhere else, on time. But none of us dawdled so intolerably
about the business of being born as did my baby sister.
We sometimes amused ourselves, during those endless,
stifling weeks, by picturing the baby sitting within in the
safe, warm dark, bitterly regretting the necessity of becoming a part of our chaos and stubbornly putting it off
as long as possible. I understood her perfectly and con-
gratulated her on showing such good sense so soon. Death,
however, sat as purposefully at my father's bedside as
life stirred within my mother's womb and it was harder
to understand why he so lingered in that long shadow.
It seemed that he had bent, and for a long time, too, all
of his energies towards dying. Now death was ready for
him but my father held back.

All of Harlem, indeed, seemed to be infected by waiting. I had never before known it to be so violently still.
Racial tensions throughout this country were exacerbated
during the early years of the war, partly because the labor
market brought together hundreds of thousands of ill-

prepared people and partly because Negro soldiers, re-
gardless of where they were born, received their military
training in the south. What happened in defense plants
and army camps had repercussions, naturally, in every
Negro ghetto. The situation in Harlem had grown bad
enough for clergymen, policemen, educators, politicians,
and social workers to assert in one breath that there was
no "crime wave" and to offer, in the very next breath,
suggestions as to how to combat it. These suggestions
always seemed to involve playgrounds, despite the fact
that racial skirmishes were occurring in the playgrounds,
too. Playground or not, crime wave or not, the Harlem
police force had been augmented in March, and the unrest
grew — perhaps, in fact, partly as a result of the ghetto's
instinctive hatred of policemen. Perhaps the most revealing news item, out of the steady parade of reports of
muggings, stabbings, shootings, assaults, gang wars, and
accusations of police brutality, is the item concerning six
Negro girls who set upon a white girl in the subway because, as they all too accurately put it, she was stepping
on their toes. Indeed she was, all over the nation.

I had never before been so aware of policemen, on foot,
on horseback, on corners, everywhere, always two by two.
Nor had I ever been so aware of small knots of people.
They were on stoops and on corners and in doorways, and
what was striking about them, I think, was that they did
not seem to be talking. Never, when I passed these
groups, did the usual sound of a curse or a laugh ring out
and neither did there seem to be any hum of gossip. There
was certainly, on the other hand, occurring between them
communication extraordinarily intense. Another thing
that was striking was the unexpected diversity of the

people who made up these groups. Usually, for example, one would see a group of sharpies standing on the street corner, jiving the passing chicks; or a group of older men, usually, for some reason, in the vicinity of a barber shop, discussing baseball scores, or the numbers, or making rather chilling observations about women they had known. Women, in a general way, tended to be seen less often together — unless they were church women, or very young girls, or prostitutes met together for an unprofessional instant. But that summer I saw the strangest combinations: large, respectable, churchly matrons standing on the stoops or the corners with their hair tied up, together with a girl in sleazy satin whose face bore the marks of gin and the razor, or heavy-set, abrupt, no-nonsense older men, in company with the most disreputable and fanatical "race" men, or these same "race" men with the sharpies, or these sharpies with the churchly women. Seventh Day Adventists and Methodists and Spiritualists seemed to be hobnobbing with Holyrollers and they were all, alike, entangled with the most flagrant disbelievers; something heavy in their stance seemed to indicate that they had all, incredibly, seen a common vision, and on each face there seemed to be the same strange, bitter shadow.

The churchly women and the matter-of-fact, no-nonsense men had children in the Army. The sleazy girls they talked to had lovers there, the sharpies and the "race" men had friends and brothers there. It would have demanded an unquestioning patriotism, happily as uncommon in this country as it is undesirable, for these people not to have been disturbed by the bitter letters they received, by the newspaper stories they read, not to have been enraged by the posters, then to be found all over

New York, which described the Japanese as "yellow-bellied Japs." It was only the "race" men, to be sure, who spoke ceaselessly of being revenged — how this vengeance was to be exacted was not clear — for the indignities and dangers suffered by Negro boys in uniform; but everybody felt a directionless, hopeless bitterness, as well as that panic which can scarcely be suppressed when one knows that a human being one loves is beyond one's reach, and in danger. This helplessness and this gnawing uneasiness does something, at length, to even the toughest mind. Perhaps the best way to sum all this up is to say that the people I knew felt, mainly, a peculiar kind of relief when they knew that their boys were being shipped out of the south, to do battle overseas. It was, perhaps, like feeling that the most dangerous part of a dangerous journey had been passed and that now, even if death should come, it would come with honor and without the complicity of their countrymen. Such a death would be, in short, a fact with which one could hope to live.

It was on the 28th of July, which I believe was a Wednesday, that I visited my father for the first time during his illness and for the last time in his life. The moment I saw him I knew why I had put off this visit so long. I had told my mother that I did not want to see him because I hated him. But this was not true. It was only that I *had* hated him and I wanted to hold on to this hatred. I did not want to look on him as a ruin: it was not a ruin I had hated. I imagine that one of the reasons people cling to their hates so stubbornly is because they sense, once hate is gone, that they will be forced to deal with pain.

We traveled out to him, his older sister and myself,

to what seemed to be the very end of a very Long Island. It was hot and dusty and we wrangled, my aunt and I, all the way out, over the fact that I had recently begun to smoke and, as she said, to give myself airs. But I knew that she wrangled with me because she could not bear to face the fact of her brother's dying. Neither could I endure the reality of her despair, her unstated bafflement as to what had happened to her brother's life, and her own. So we wrangled and I smoked and from time to time she fell into a heavy reverie. Covertly, I watched her face, which was the face of an old woman; it had fallen in, the eyes were sunken and lightless; soon she would be dying, too.

In my childhood — it had not been so long ago — I had thought her beautiful. She had been quick-witted and quick-moving and very generous with all the children and each of her visits had been an event. At one time one of my brothers and myself had thought of running away to live with her. Now she could no longer produce out of her handbag some unexpected and yet familiar delight. She made me feel pity and revulsion and fear. It was awful to realize that she no longer caused me to feel affection. The closer we came to the hospital the more querulous she became and at the same time, naturally, grew more dependent on me. Between pity and guilt and fear I began to feel that there was another me trapped in my skull like a jack-in-the-box who might escape my control at any moment and fill the air with screaming.

She began to cry the moment we entered the room and she saw him lying there, all shriveled and still, like a little black monkey. The great, gleaming apparatus which fed him and would have compelled him to be still even if

he had been able to move brought to mind, not benefi-
cence, but torture; the tubes entering his arm made me
think of pictures I had seen when a child, of Gulliver, tied
down by the pygmies on that island. My aunt wept and
wept, there was a whistling sound in my father's throat;
nothing was said; he could not speak. I wanted to take
his hand, to say something. But I do not know what I
could have said, even if he could have heard me. He
was not really in that room with us, he had at last really
embarked on his journey; and though my aunt told me
that he said he was going to meet Jesus, I did not hear
anything except that whistling in his throat. The doctor
came back and we left, into that unbearable train again,
and home. In the morning came the telegram saying that
he was dead. Then the house was suddenly full of relatives, friends, hysteria, and confusion and I quickly left
my mother and the children to the care of those impressive
women, who, in Negro communities at least, automatically
appear at times of bereavement armed with lotions, prov-
erbs, and patience, and an ability to cook. I went downtown. By the time I returned, later the same day, my
mother had been carried to the hospital and the baby had
been born.

III

For my father's funeral I had nothing black to wear and
this posed a nagging problem all day long. It was one of
those problems, simple, or impossible of solution, to which
the mind insanely clings in order to avoid the mind's real
trouble. I spent most of that day at the downtown apart-
ment of a girl I knew, celebrating my birthday with whis-

key and wondering what to wear that night. When planning a birthday celebration one naturally does not expect that it will be up against competition from a funeral and this girl had anticipated taking me out that night, for a big dinner and a night club afterwards. Sometime during the course of that long day we decided that we would go out anyway, when my father's funeral service was over. I imagine *I* decided it, since, as the funeral hour approached, it became clearer and clearer to me that I would not know what to do with myself when it was over. The girl, stifling her very lively concern as to the possible effects of the whiskey on one of my father's chief mourners, concentrated on being conciliatory and practically helpful. She found a black shirt for me somewhere and ironed it and, dressed in the darkest pants and jacket I owned, and slightly drunk, I made my way to my father's funeral.

The chapel was full, but not packed, and very quiet. There were, mainly, my father's relatives, and his children, and here and there I saw faces I had not seen since childhood, the faces of my father's one-time friends. They were very dark and solemn now, seeming somehow to suggest that they had known all along that something like this would happen. Chief among the mourners was my aunt, who had quarreled with my father all his life; by which I do not mean to suggest that her mourning was insincere or that she had not loved him. I suppose that she was one of the few people in the world who had, and their incessant quarreling proved precisely the strength of the tie that bound them. The only other person in the world, as far as I knew, whose relationship to my father rivaled my aunt's in depth was my mother, who was not there.

It seemed to me, of course, that it was a very long funeral. But it was, if anything, a rather shorter funeral than most, nor, since there were no overwhelming, uncontrollable expressions of grief, could it be called — if I dare to use the word — successful. The minister who preached my father's funeral sermon was one of the few my father had still been seeing as he neared his end. He presented to us in his sermon a man whom none of us had ever seen — a man thoughtful, patient, and forbearing, a Christian inspiration to all who knew him, and a model for his children. And no doubt the children, in their disturbed and guilty state, were almost ready to believe this; he had been remote enough to be anything and, anyway, the shock of the incontrovertible, that it was really our father lying up there in that casket, prepared the mind for anything. His sister moaned and this grief-stricken moaning was taken as corroboration. The other faces held a dark, non-committal thoughtfulness. This was not the man they had known, but they had scarcely expected to be confronted with *him;* this was, in a sense deeper than questions of fact, the man they had not known, and the man they had not known may have been the real one. The real man, whoever he had been, had suffered and now he was dead: this was all that was sure and all that mattered now. Every man in the chapel hoped that when his hour came he, too, would be eulogized, which is to say forgiven, and that all of his lapses, greeds, errors, and strayings from the truth would be invested with coherence and looked upon with charity. This was perhaps the last thing human beings could give each other and it was what they demanded, after all, of the Lord. Only the Lord saw the midnight tears, only He was present when one of His children, moaning and wringing hands, paced up and down the room. When one slapped one's child in anger the recoil in the heart reverberated through heaven and became part of the pain of the universe. And when the children were hungry and sullen and distrustful and one watched them, daily, growing wilder, and further away, and running headlong into danger, it was the Lord who knew what the charged heart endured as the strap was laid to the backside; the Lord alone who knew what one *would* have said if one had had, like the Lord, the gift of the living word. It was the Lord who knew of the impossibility every parent in that room faced: how to prepare the child for the day when the child would be despised and how to *create* in the child — by what means? — a stronger antidote to this poison than one had found for oneself. The avenues, side streets, bars, billiard halls, hospitals, police stations, and even the playgrounds of Harlem — not to mention the houses of correction, the jails, and the morgue — testified to the potency of the poison while remaining silent as to the efficacy of whatever antidote, irresistibly raising the question of whether or not such an antidote existed; raising, which was worse, the question of whether or not an antidote was desirable; perhaps poison should be fought with poison. With these several schisms in the mind and with more terrors in the heart than could be named, it was better not to judge the man who had gone down under an impossible burden. It was better to remember: *Thou knowest this man's fall; but thou knowest not his wrassling.*

While the preacher talked and I watched the children — years of changing their diapers, scrubbing them, slapping them, taking them to school, and scolding them had

had the perhaps inevitable result of making me love them, though I am not sure I knew this then — my mind was busily breaking out with a rash of disconnected impressions. Snatches of popular songs, indecent jokes, bits of books I had read, movie sequences, faces, voices, political issues — I thought I was going mad; all these impressions suspended, as it were, in the solution of the faint nausea produced in me by the heat and liquor. For a moment I had the impression that my alcoholic breath, inefficiently disguised with chewing gum, filled the entire chapel. Then someone began singing one of my father's favorite songs and, abruptly, I was with him, sitting on his knee, in the hot, enormous, crowded church which was the first church we attended. It was the Abyssinia Baptist Church on 138th Street. We had not gone there long. With this image, a host of others came. I had forgotten, in the rage of my growing up, how proud my father had been of me when I was little. Apparently, I had had a voice and my father had liked to show me off before the members of the church. I had forgotten what he had looked like when he was pleased but now I remembered that he had always been grinning with pleasure when my solos ended. I even remembered certain expressions on his face when he teased my mother — had he loved her? I would never know. And when had it all begun to change? For now it seemed that he had not always been cruel. I remembered being taken for a haircut and scraping my knee on the footrest of the barber's chair and I remembered my father's face as he soothed my crying and applied the stinging iodine. Then I remembered our fights, fights which had been of the worst possible kind because my technique had been silence.

I remembered the one time in all our life together when we had really spoken to each other.

It was on a Sunday and it must have been shortly before I left home. We were walking, just the two of us, in our usual silence, to or from church. I was in high school and had been doing a lot of writing and I was, at about this time, the editor of the high school magazine. But I had also been a Young Minister and had been preaching from the pulpit. Lately, I had been taking fewer engagements and preached as rarely as possible. It was said in the church, quite truthfully, that I was "cooling off."

My father asked me abruptly, "You'd rather write than preach, wouldn't you?"

I was astonished at his question — because it was a real question. I answered, "Yes."

That was all we said. It was awful to remember that that was all we had *ever* said.

The casket now was opened and the mourners were being led up the aisle to look for the last time on the deceased. The assumption was that the family was too overcome with grief to be allowed to make this journey alone and I watched while my aunt was led to the casket and, muffled in black, and shaking, led back to her seat. I disapproved of forcing the children to look on their dead father, considering that the shock of his death, or, more truthfully, the shock of death as a reality, was already a little more than a child could bear, but my judgment in this matter had been overruled and there they were, bewildered and frightened and very small, being led, one by one, to the casket. But there is also something very gallant about children at such moments.

It has something to do with their silence and gravity and with the fact that one cannot help them. Their legs, somehow, seem *exposed*, so that it is at once incredible and terribly clear that their legs are all they have to hold them up.

I had not wanted to go to the casket myself and I certainly had not wished to be led there, but there was no way of avoiding either of these forms. One of the deacons led me up and I looked on my father's face. I cannot say that it looked like him at all. His blackness had been equivocated by powder and there was no suggestion in that casket of what his power had or could have been. He was simply an old man dead, and it was hard to believe that he had ever given anyone either joy or pain. Yet, his life filled that room. Further up the avenue his wife was holding his newborn child. Life and death so close together, and love and hatred, and right and wrong, said something to me which I did not want to hear concerning man, concerning the life of man.

After the funeral, while I was downtown desperately celebrating my birthday, a Negro soldier, in the lobby of the Hotel Braddock, got into a fight with a white policeman over a Negro girl. Negro girls, white policemen, in or out of uniform, and Negro males — in or out of uniform — were part of the furniture of the lobby of the Hotel Braddock and this was certainly not the first time such an incident had occurred. It was destined, however, to receive an unprecedented publicity, for the fight between the policeman and the soldier ended with the shooting of the soldier. Rumor, flowing immediately to the streets outside, stated that the soldier had been shot in the back, an instantaneous and revealing invention, and that the soldier had died protecting a Negro woman. The facts were somewhat different — for example, the soldier had not been shot in the back, and was not dead, and the girl seems to have been as dubious a symbol of woman-hood as her white counterpart in Georgia usually is, but no one was interested in the facts. They preferred the invention because this invention expressed and corrobo-rated their hates and fears so perfectly. It is just as well to remember that people are always doing this. Perhaps many of those legends, including Christianity, to which the world clings began their conquest of the world with just some such concerted surrender to distortion. The effect, in Harlem, of this particular legend was like the effect of a lit match in a tin of gasoline. The mob gathered before the doors of the Hotel Braddock simply began to swell and to spread in every direction, and Harlem ex-ploded.

The mob did not cross the ghetto lines. It would have been easy, for example, to have gone over Morningside Park on the west side or to have crossed the Grand Central railroad tracks at 125th Street on the east side, to wreak havoc in white neighborhoods. The mob seems to have been mainly interested in something more potent and real than the white face, that is, in white power, and the prin-cipal damage done during the riot of the summer of 1943 was to white business establishments in Harlem. It might have been a far bloodier story, of course, if, at the hour the riot began, these establishments had still been open. From the Hotel Braddock the mob fanned out, east and west along 125th Street, and for the entire length of Lenox, Seventh, and Eighth avenues. Along each of these avenues, and along each major side street — 116th, 125th, 135th, and so on — bars, stores, pawnshops, restaurants, even little luncheonettes had been smashed open and entered and looted — looted, it might be added, with more haste than efficiency. The shelves really looked as though a bomb had struck them. Cans of beans and soup and dog food, along with toilet paper, corn flakes, sardines and milk tumbled every which way, and abandoned cash registers and cases of beer leaned crazily out of the splintered windows and were strewn along the avenues. Sheets, blankets, and clothing of every description formed a kind of path, as though people had dropped them while running. I truly had not realized that Harlem *had* so many stores until I saw them all smashed open; the first time the word *wealth* ever entered my mind in relation to Harlem was when I saw it scattered in the streets. But one's first, incongruous impression of plenty was countered immediately by an impression of waste. None of this was doing anybody any good. It would have been better to have left the plate glass as it had been and the goods lying in the stores.

It would have been better, but it would also have been intolerable, for Harlem had needed something to smash. To smash something is the ghetto's chronic need. Most of the time it is the members of the ghetto who smash each other, and themselves. But as long as the ghetto walls are standing there will always come a moment when these outlets do not work. That summer, for example, it was not enough to get into a fight on Lenox Avenue, or curse out one's cronies in the barber shops. If ever, indeed, the violence which fills Harlem's churches, pool halls, and bars erupts outward in a more direct fashion,

Harlem and its citizens are likely to vanish in an apocalyptic flood. That this is not likely to happen is due to a great many reasons, most hidden and powerful among them the Negro's real relation to the white American. This relation prohibits, simply, anything as uncomplicated and satisfactory as pure hatred. In order really to hate white people, one has to blot so much out of the mind — and the heart — that this hatred itself becomes an exhausting and self-destructive pose. But this does not mean, on the other hand, that love comes easily: the white world is too powerful, too complacent, too ready with gratuitous humiliation, and, above all, too ignorant and too innocent for that. One is absolutely forced to make perpetual qualifications and one's own reactions are always canceling each other out. It is this, really, which has driven so many people mad, both white and black. One is always in the position of having to decide between amputation and gangrene. Amputation is swift but time may prove that the amputation was not necessary — or one may delay the amputation too long. Gangrene is slow, but it is impossible to be sure that one is reading one's symptoms right. The idea of going through life as a cripple is more than one can bear, and equally unbearable is the risk of swelling up slowly, in agony, with poison. And the trouble, finally, is that the risks are real even if the choices do not exist.

"But as for me and my house," my father had said, "we will serve the Lord." I wondered, as we drove him to his resting place, what this line had meant for him. I had heard him preach it many times. I had preached it once myself, proudly giving it an interpretation different from my father's. Now the whole thing came back to me, as

though my father and I were on our way to Sunday school
and I were memorizing the golden text: *And if it seem
evil unto you to serve the Lord, choose you this day whom
you will serve; whether the gods which your fathers served
that were on the other side of the flood, or the gods of the
Amorites, in whose land ye dwell: but as for me and my
house, we will serve the Lord.* I suspected in these familiar lines a meaning which had never been there for me
before. All of my father's texts and songs, which I had
decided were meaningless, were arranged before me at
his death like empty bottles, waiting to hold the meaning
which life would give them for me. This was his legacy:
nothing is ever escaped. That bleakly memorable morning
I hated the unbelievable streets and the Negroes and
whites who had, equally, made them that way. But I knew
that it was folly, as my father would have said, this bitterness was folly. It was necessary to hold on to the things
that mattered. The dead man mattered, the new life
mattered; blackness and whiteness did not matter; to
believe that they did was to acquiesce in one's own destruction. Hatred, which could destroy so much, never
failed to destroy the man who hated and this was an
immutable law.

It began to seem that one would have to hold in the
mind forever two ideas which seemed to be in opposition.
The first idea was acceptance, the acceptance, totally
without rancor, of life as it is, and men as they are: in the
light of this idea, it goes without saying that injustice is a
commonplace. But this did not mean that one could be
complacent, for the second idea was of equal power: that
one must never, in one's own life, accept these injustices
as commonplace but must fight them with all one's

strength. This fight begins, however, in the heart and it now had been laid to my charge to keep my own heart free of hatred and despair. This intimation made my heart heavy and, now that my father was irrecoverable, I wished that he had been beside me so that I could have searched his face for the answers which only the future would give me now.

PART THREE

Encounter on the Seine: Black Meets Brown

In Paris nowadays it is rather more difficult for an American Negro to become a really successful entertainer than it is rumored to have been some thirty years ago. For one thing, champagne has ceased to be drunk out of slippers, and the frivolously colored thousand-franc note is neither as elastic nor as freely spent as it was in the 1920's. The musicians and singers who are here now must work very hard indeed to acquire the polish and style which will land them in the big time. Bearing witness to this eternally tantalizing possibility, performers whose eminence is unchallenged, like Duke Ellington or Louis Armstrong, occasionally pass through. Some of their ambitious followers are in or near the big time already; others are gaining reputations which have yet to be tested in the States. Gordon Heath, who will be remembered for his performances as the embattled soldier in Broadway's *Deep Are the Roots* some seasons back, sings ballads nightly in his own night club on the Rue L'Abbaye; and everyone who comes to Paris these days sooner or later discovers Chez Inez, a night club in the Latin Quarter run by a singer named Inez Cavanaugh, which specializes in fried chicken and jazz. It is at Chez Inez that many an unknown first performs in public, going on thereafter, if not always to greater triumphs, at least to other night clubs, and possibly landing a contract to tour the Riviera during the spring and summer.

In general, only the Negro entertainers are able to maintain a useful and unquestioning comradeship with other Negroes. Their nonperforming, colored countrymen are, nearly to a man, incomparably more isolated, and it must be conceded that this isolation is deliberate. It is estimated that there are five hundred American Negroes living in this city, the vast majority of them veterans studying on the G.I. Bill. They are studying everything from the Sorbonne's standard *Cours de Civilisation Française* to abnormal psychology, brain surgery, music, fine arts, and literature. Their isolation from each other is not difficult to understand if one bears in mind the axiom, unquestioned by American landlords, that Negroes are happy only when they are kept together. Those driven to break this pattern by leaving the U.S. ghettos not merely have effected a social and physical leave-taking but also have been precipitated into cruel psychological warfare. It is altogether inevitable that past humiliations should become associated not only with one's traditional oppressors but also with one's traditional kinfolk.

Thus the sight of a face from home is not invariably a source of joy, but can also quite easily become a source of embarrassment or rage. The American Negro in Paris is forced at last to exercise an undemocratic discrimination rarely practiced by Americans, that of judging his people, duck by duck, and distinguishing them one from another. Through this deliberate isolation, through lack of numbers, and above all through his own overwhelming need to be, as it were, forgotten, the American Negro in Paris is very nearly the invisible man.

The wariness with which he regards his colored kin is a natural extension of the wariness with which he regards all of his countrymen. At the beginning, certainly, he cherishes rather exaggerated hopes of the French. His white countrymen, by and large, fail to justify his fears, partly because the social climate does not encourage an outward display of racial bigotry, partly out of their awareness of being ambassadors, and finally, I should think, because they are themselves relieved at being no longer forced to think in terms of color. There remains, nevertheless, in the encounter of white Americans and Negro Americans the high potential of an awkward or an ugly situation.

The white American regards his darker brother through the distorting screen created by a lifetime of conditioning. He is accustomed to regard him either as a needy and deserving martyr or as the soul of rhythm, but he is more than a little intimidated to find this stranger so many miles from home. At first he tends instinctively, whatever his intelligence may belatedly clamor, to take it as a reflection on his personal honor and good-will; and at the same time, with that winning generosity, at once good-natured and uneasy, which characterizes Americans, he would like to establish communication, and sympathy, with his compatriot. "And how do *you* feel about it?" he would like to ask, "it" being anything — the Russians, Betty Grable, the Place de la Concorde. The trouble here is that any "it," so tentatively offered, may suddenly become loaded and vibrant with tension, creating in the air between the two thus met an intolerable atmosphere of danger.

The Negro, on the other hand, via the same conditioning which constricts the outward gesture of the whites, has learned to anticipate: as the mouth opens he divines what the tongue will utter. He has had time, too, long before he came to Paris, to reflect on the absolute and personally expensive futility of taking any one of his countrymen to task for his status in America, or of hoping to convey to them any of his experience. The American Negro and white do not, therefore, discuss the past, except in considerately guarded snatches. Both are quite willing, and indeed quite wise, to remark instead the considerably overrated impressiveness of the Eiffel Tower.

The Eiffel Tower has naturally long since ceased to divert the French, who consider that all Negroes arrive from America, trumpet-laden and twinkle-toed, bearing scars so unutterably painful that all of the glories of the French Republic may not suffice to heal them. This indignant generosity poses problems of its own, which, language and custom being what they are, are not so easily averted.

The European tends to avoid the really monumental confusion which might result from an attempt to apprehend the relationship of the forty-eight states to one another, clinging instead to such information as is afforded by radio, press, and film, to anecdotes considered to be illustrative of American life, and to the myth that we have ourselves perpetuated. The result, in conversation, is rather like seeing one's back yard reproduced with extreme fidelity, but in such a perspective that it becomes a place which one has never seen or visited, which never has existed, and which never can exist. The Negro is forced to say "Yes" to many a difficult question, and yet to deny the conclusion to which his answers seem to point. His past, he now realizes, has not been simply a series of ropes and bonfires and humiliations, but something vastly more complex, which, as he thinks painfully, "It was much worse than that," was also, he irrationally feels, something much better. As it is useless to excoriate his countrymen, it is galling now to be pitied as a victim, to accept this ready sympathy which is limited only by its failure to accept him as an American. He finds himself involved, in another language, in the same old battle: the battle for his own identity. To accept the reality of his being an American becomes a matter involving his integrity and his greatest hopes, for only by accepting this reality can he hope to make articulate to himself or to others the uniqueness of his experience, and to set free the spirit so long anonymous and caged.

The ambivalence of his status is thrown into relief by his encounters with the Negro students from France's colonies who live in Paris. The French African comes from a region and a way of life which — at least from the American point of view — is exceedingly primitive, and where exploitation takes more naked forms. In Paris, the African Negro's status, conspicuous and subtly inconvenient, is that of a colonial; and he leads here the intangibly precarious life of someone abruptly and recently uprooted. His bitterness is unlike that of his American kinsman in that it is not so treacherously likely to be turned against himself. He has, not so very many miles away, a homeland to which his relationship, no less than his responsibility, is overwhelmingly clear: His country must be given — or it must seize — its freedom. This bitter ambition is shared by his fellow colonials, with whom he has a common language, and whom he has no wish whatever to avoid; without whose sustenance, indeed, he would be almost altogether lost in Paris. They live in groups together, in the same neighborhoods, in student hotels and under conditions which cannot fail to impress the American as almost unendurable.

Yet what the American is seeing is not simply the poverty of the student but the enormous gap between the European and American standards of living. *All* of the students in the Latin Quarter live in ageless, sinister-looking hotels; they are all forced continually to choose between cigarettes and cheese at lunch.

It is true that the poverty and anger which the American Negro sees must be related to Europe and not to America. Yet, as he wishes for a moment that he were home again, where at least the terrain is familiar, there begins to race within him, like the despised beat of the tom-tom, echoes of a past which he has not yet been able to utilize, intimations of a responsibility which he has not yet been able to face. He begins to conjecture how much he has gained and lost during his long sojourn in the American republic. The African before him has endured privation, injustice, medieval cruelty; but the African has not yet endured the utter alienation of himself from his people and his past. His mother did not sing "Sometimes I Feel Like a Motherless Child," and he has not, all his life long, ached for acceptance in a culture which pronounced straight hair and white skin the only acceptable beauty.

They face each other, the Negro and the African, over a gulf of three hundred years — an alienation too vast to be conquered in an evening's good-will, too heavy and too double-edged ever to be trapped in speech. This alienation causes the Negro to recognize that he is a hybrid. Not a physical hybrid merely: in every aspect of his living he betrays the memory of the auction block and the impact of the happy ending. In white Americans he finds reflected — repeated, as it were, in a higher key — his tensions, his terrors, his tenderness. Dimly and for the first time, there begins to fall into perspective the nature of the roles they have played in the lives and history of each other. Now he is bone of their bone, flesh of their flesh; they have loved and hated and obsessed and feared each other and his blood is in their soil. Therefore he cannot deny them, nor can they ever be divorced.

The American Negro cannot explain to the African what surely seems in himself to be a want of manliness, of racial pride, a maudlin ability to forgive. It is difficult to make clear that he is not seeking to forfeit his birthright as a black man, but that, on the contrary, it is precisely this birthright which he is struggling to recognize and make articulate. Perhaps it now occurs to him that in this need to establish himself in relation to his past he is most American, that this depthless alienation from oneself and one's people is, in sum, the American experience.

Yet one day he will face his home again; nor can he realistically expect to find overwhelming changes. In America, it is true, the appearance is perpetually changing, each generation greeting with short-lived exultation yet more dazzling additions to our renowned façade. But the ghetto, anxiety, bitterness, and guilt continue to breed their indescribable complex of tensions. What time will bring Americans is at last their own identity. It is on this dangerous voyage and in the same boat that the American Negro will make peace with himself and with the voiceless many thousands gone before him.

A Question of Identity

The American student colony in Paris is a social phenomenon so amorphous as to at once demand and defy the generality. One is far from being in the position of finding not enough to say — one finds far too much, and everything one finds is contradictory. What one wants to know at bottom, is what *they* came to find: to which question there are — at least — as many answers as there are faces at the café tables.

The assumed common denominator, which is their military experience, does not shed on this question as much light as one might hope. For one thing, it becomes impossible, the moment one thinks about it, to predicate the existence of a *common* experience. The moment one thinks about it, it becomes apparent that there is no such thing. That experience is a private, and a very largely speechless affair is the principal truth, perhaps, to which the colony under discussion bears witness — though the aggressively unreadable face which they, collectively, present also suggests the more disturbing possibility that experience may perfectly well be meaningless. This loaded speculation aside, it is certainly true that whatever this experience has done to them, or for them, whatever the effect has been, is, or will be, is a question to which no one has yet given any strikingly coherent answer. Military experience does not, furthermore, necessarily mean experience of battle, so that the student colony's common denominator reduces itself to nothing more than the fact that all of its members have spent some time in uniform. This is the common denominator of their entire generation, of which the majority is not to be found in Paris, or, for that matter, in Europe. One is at the outset, therefore, forbidden to assume that the fact of having surrendered to the necessary anonymity of uniform, or of having undergone the shock of battle, was enough to occasion this flight from home. The best that one can do by way of uniting these so disparate identities is simply to accept, without comment, the fact of their military experience, without questioning its extent; and, further, to suggest that they form, by virtue of their presence here, a somewhat unexpected minority. Unlike the majority of their fellows, who were simply glad to get back home, these have elected to tarry in the Old World, among scenes and people unimaginably removed from anything they have known. They are willing, apparently, at least for a season, to endure the wretched Parisian plumbing, the public baths, the Paris age, and dirt — to pursue some end, mysterious and largely inarticulate, arbitrarily summed up in the verb *to study*.

Arbitrarily, because, however hard the ex-GI is studying, it is very difficult to believe that it was only for this reason that he traveled so far. He is not, usually, studying anything which he couldn't study at home, in far greater comfort. (We are limiting ourselves, for the moment, to those people who are — more or less seriously — studying, as opposed to those, to be considered later, who are merely gold-bricking.) The people, for example, who are studying painting, which seems, until one looks around, the best possible subject to be studying here, are not studying, after all, with Picasso, or Matisse — they are studying with teachers of the same caliber as those they would have found in the States. They are treated by these teachers with the same highhandedness, and they accept their dicta with the very same measure of American salt. Nor can it be said that they produce canvases of any greater interest than those to be found along Washington Square, or in the cold-water flats of New York's lower east side. There is, *au contraire,* more than a little truth to the contention that the east side has a certain edge over Montparnasse, and this in spite of the justly renowned Paris light. If we tentatively use — purely by virtue of his numbers — the student painter as the nearest possible approach to a "typical" student, we find that his motives for coming to Paris are anything but clear. One is forced to suppose that it was nothing more than the legend of Paris, not infrequently at its most vulgar and superficial level. It was certainly no love for French tradition, whatever, indeed, in his mind, that tradition may be; and, in any case, since he is himself without a tradition, he is ill equipped to deal with the traditions of any other people. It was no love for their language, which he doesn't, beyond the most inescapable necessities, speak; nor was it any love for their history, his grasp of French history being yet more feeble than his understanding of his own. It was no love for the monuments, cathedrals, palaces, shrines, for which, again, nothing in his experience prepares him, and to which, when he is not totally indifferent, he brings only the hurried bewilderment of the tourist. It was not even any particular admiration, or sympathy for the French, or, at least, none strong enough to bear the strain of actual contact. He may, at home, have admired their movies, in which case, confronting the reality, he tends to feel a little taken in. Those images created by Marcel Carné, for example, prove themselves treacherous precisely because they are so exact. The sordid French hotel room, so admirably detailed by the camera, speaking, in its quaintness, and distance, so beautifully of romance, undergoes a sea-change, becomes a room positively hostile to romance, once it is oneself, and not Jean Gabin, who lives there. This is the difference, simply, between what one desires and what the reality insists on — which difference we will not pursue except to observe that, since the reasons which brought the student here are so romantic, and incoherent, he has come, in effect, to a city which exists only in his mind. He cushions himself, so it would seem, against the shock of reality, by refusing for a very long time to recognize Paris at all, but clinging instead to its image. This is the reason, perhaps, that Paris for so long fails to make any mark on him; and may also be why, when the tension between the real and the imagined can no longer be supported, so many people undergo a species of breakdown, or take the first boat home.

For Paris is, according to its legend, the city where everyone loses his head, and his morals, lives through at least one *histoire d'amour*, ceases, quite, to arrive anywhere on time, and thumbs his nose at the Puritans — the city, in brief, where all become drunken on the fine old air of freedom. This legend, in the fashion of legends, has this much to support it, that it is not at all difficult to see how it got started. It is limited, as legends are limited, by being — literally — unlivable, and by referring to the past. It is perhaps not amazing, therefore, that this legend

appears to have virtually nothing to do with the life of
Paris itself, with the lives, that is, of the natives, to whom
the city, no less than the legend, belong. The charm of
this legend proves itself capable of withstanding the most
improbable excesses of the French bureaucracy, the
weirdest vagaries of the *concierge*, the fantastic rents paid
for uncomfortable apartments, the discomfort itself, and,
even, the great confusion and despair which is reflected
in French politics — and in French faces. More, the
legend operates to place all of the inconveniences endured
by the foreigner, to say nothing of the downright misery
which is the lot of many of the natives, in the gentle glow
of the picturesque, and the absurd; so that, finally, it is
perfectly possible to be enamored of Paris while remaining totally indifferent, or even hostile to the French. And
this is made possible by the one person in Paris whom the
legend seems least to affect, who is not living it at all,
that is, the Parisian himself. He, with his impenetrable
politesse, and with techniques unspeakably more direct,
keeps the traveler at an unmistakable arm's length. Unlucky indeed, as well as rare, the traveler who thirsts to
know the lives of the people — the people don't want him
in their lives. Neither does the Parisian exhibit the faintest
personal interest, or curiosity, concerning the life, or habits,
of any stranger. So long as he keeps within the law, which,
after all, most people have sufficient ingenuity to do, he
may stand on his head, for all the Parisian cares. It is this
arrogant indifference on the part of the Parisian, with its
unpredictable effects on the traveler, which makes so
splendid the Paris air, to say nothing whatever of the
exhilarating effect it has on the Paris scene.

The American student lives here, then, in a kind of

social limbo. He is allowed, and he gratefully embraces irresponsibility; and, at the same time, since he is an American, he is invested with power, whether or not he likes it, however he may choose to confirm or deny it. Though the students of any nation, in Paris, are allowed irresponsibility, few seem to need it as desperately as Americans seem to need it; and none, naturally, move in the same aura of power, which sets up in the general breast a perceptible anxiety, and wonder, and a perceptible resentment. This is the "catch," for the American, in the Paris freedom: that he becomes here a kind of revenant to Europe, the future of which continent, it may be, is in his hands. The problems proceeding from the distinction he thus finds thrust upon him might not, for a sensibility less definitively lonely, frame so painful a dilemma: but the American wishes to be liked *as a person,* an implied distinction which makes perfect sense to him, and none whatever to the European. What the American means is that he does not want to be confused with the Marshall Plan, Hollywood, the Yankee dollar, television, or Senator McCarthy. What the European, in a thoroughly exasperating innocence, assumes is that the American cannot, of course, be divorced from the so diverse phenomena which make up his country, and that he is willing, and able, to clarify the American conundrum. If the American cannot do this, his despairing aspect seems to say, who, under heaven, can? This moment, which instinctive ingenuity delays as long as possible, nevertheless arrives, and punctuates the Paris honeymoon. It is the moment, so to speak, when one leaves the Paris of legend and finds oneself in the real and difficult Paris of the present. At this moment Paris ceases to be a city dedicated to *la vie bohème,* and becomes one of the cities of Europe. At this point, too, it may be suggested, the legend of Paris has done its deadly work, which is, perhaps, so to stun the traveler with freedom that he begins to long for the prison of home — home then becoming the place where questions are not asked.

It is at this point, precisely, that many and many a student packs his bags for home. The transformation which can be effected, in less than a year, in the attitude and aspirations of the youth who has divorced himself from the crudities of main street in order to be married with European finesse is, to say the very least, astounding. His brief period of enchantment having ended, he cannot wait, it seems, to look again on his native land — the virtues of which, if not less crude, have also become, abruptly, *simple,* and *vital.* With the air of a man who has but barely escaped tumbling headlong into the bottomless pit, he tells you that he can scarcely wait to leave this city, which has been revealed to the eye of his maturity as old, dirty, crumbling, and dead. The people who were, when he arrived at Le Havre, the heirs of the world's richest culture, the possessors of the world's largest *esprit,* are really decadent, penurious, self-seeking, and false, with no trace of American spontaneity, and lacking in the least gratitude for American favors. Only America is alive, only Americans are doing anything worth mentioning in the arts, or in any other field of human activity: to America, only, the future belongs. Whereas, but only yesterday, to confess a fondness for anything American was to be suspected of the most indefensible jingoism, to suggest today that Europe is not all black is to place oneself under the suspicion of harboring treasonable longings. The vio-

lence of his embrace of things American is embarrassing,
not only because one is not quite prepared to follow his
admirable example, but also because it is impossible not
to suspect that his present acceptance of his country is no
less romantic, and unreal, than his earlier rejection. It is
as easy, after all, and as meaningless, to embrace un-
critically the cultural sterility of main street as it is to
decry it. Both extremes avoid the question of whether or
not main street is really sterile, avoid, in fact — which is
the principal convenience of extremes — any questions
about main street at all. What one vainly listens for in
this cacophony of affirmation is any echo, however faint
of individual maturity. It is really quite impossible to be
affirmative about anything which one refuses to question; one is doomed to remain inarticulate about anything
which one hasn't, by an act of the imagination, made
one's own. This so suddenly affirmative student is but
changing the fashion of his innocence, nothing being
more improbable than that he is now prepared, as he
insists, to embrace his Responsibilities — the very word,
in the face of his monumental aversion to experience,
seems to shrink to the dimensions of a new, and rather
sinister, frivolity.

The student, homeward bound, has only chosen, however, to flee down the widest road. Of those who remain
here, the majority have taken roads more devious, and
incomparably better hidden — so well hidden that they
themselves are lost.

One very often finds in this category that student whose
adaptation to French life seems to have been most perfect,
and whose studies — of French art, or the drama, the

language, or the history — give him the greatest right to be here. This student has put aside chewing gum forever, he eschews the T-shirt, and the crew cut, he can only with difficulty be prevailed upon to see an American movie, and it is so patent that he is *actually* studying that his appearance at the café tables is never taken as evidence of frivolity, but only as proof of his admirable passion to study the customs of the country. One assumes that he is living as the French live — which assumption, however, is immediately challenged by the suspicion that no American *can* live as the French live, even if one could find an American who wanted to. This student lives, nevertheless, with a French family, with whom he speaks French, and takes his meals; and he knows, as some students do not, that the Place de la Bastille no longer holds the prison. He has read, or is reading, all of Racine, Proust, Gide, Sartre, and authors more obscure — in the original, naturally. He regularly visits the museums, and he considers Arletty to be the most beautiful woman and the finest actress in the world. But the world, it seems, has become the French world: he is unwilling to recognize any other. This so severely cramps the American conversational style, that one looks on this student with awe, and some shame — he is so spectacularly getting out of his European experience everything it has to give. *He* has certainly made contact with the French, and isn't wasting his time in Paris talking to people he might perfectly well have met in America. His friends are French, in the classroom, in the bistro, on the boulevard, and, of course, at home — it is only that one is sometimes driven to wonder what on earth they find to talk about. This wonder is considerably increased when, in the rare conversations he condescends

to have in English, one discovers that, certain picturesque
details aside, he seems to know no more about life in
Paris than everybody knew at home. His friends have, it
appears, leaped unscathed from the nineteenth into the
twentieth century, entirely undismayed by any of the
reverses suffered by their country. This makes them a
remarkable band indeed, but it is in vain that one attempts to discover anything more about them — their
conversation being limited, one gathers, to remarks about
French wine, witticisms concerning *l'amour*, French history, and the glories of Paris. The remarkably limited
range of their minds is matched only by their perplexing
definition of friendship, a definition which does not seem
to include any suggestion of communication, still less of
intimacy. Since, in short, the relationship of this perfectly
adapted student to the people he now so strenuously
adores is based simply on his unwillingness to allow them
any of the human attributes with which his countrymen so
confounded him at home, and since his vaunted grasp of
their history reveals itself as the merest academic plati-
tude, involving his imagination not at all, the extent of
his immersion in French life impresses one finally as the
height of artificiality, and, even, of presumption. The
most curious thing about the passion with which he has
embraced the Continent is that it seems to be nothing
more or less than a means of safeguarding his American
simplicity. He has placed himself in a kind of strongbox
of custom, and refuses to see anything in Paris which
can't be seen through a golden haze. He is thus protected
against reality, or experience, or change, and has succeeded in placing beyond the reach of corruption values
he prefers not to examine. Even his multitudinous French

friends help him to do this, for it is impossible, after all, to be friends with a mob: they are simply a cloud of faces, bearing witness to romance.

Between these two extremes, the student who embraces Home, and the student who embraces The Continent — both embraces, as we have tried to indicate, being singularly devoid of contact, to say nothing of love — there are far more gradations than can be suggested here. The American in Europe is everywhere confronted with the question of his identity, and this may be taken as the key to all the contradictions one encounters when attempting to discuss him. Certainly, for the student colony one finds no other common denominator — this is all, really, that they have in common, and they are distinguished from each other by the ways in which they come to terms, or fail to come to terms with their confusion. This prodigious question, at home so little recognized, seems, germ-like, to be vivified in the European air, and to grow disproportionately, displacing previous assurances, and producing tensions and bewilderments entirely unlooked for. It is not, moreover, a question which limits itself to those who are, so to speak, in traffic with ideas. It confronts everyone, finding everyone unprepared; it is a question with implications not easily escaped, and the attempt to escape can precipitate disaster. Our perfectly adapted student, for example, should his strongbox of custom break, may find himself hurled into that coterie of gold-bricks who form such a spectacular element of the Paris scene that they are often what the Parisian has in the foreground of his mind when he wonderingly mutters, *C'est vraiment les Américains*. The great majority of this group, having attempted, on more or less personal levels, to lose or disguise their antecedents, are reduced to a kind of rubble of compulsion. Having cast off all previous disciplines, they have also lost the shape which these disciplines made for them and have not succeeded in finding any other. Their rejection of the limitations of American society has not set them free to function in any other society, and their illusions, therefore, remain intact: they have yet to be corrupted by the notion that society is never anything less than a perfect labyrinth of limitations. They are charmed by the reflection that Paris is more than two thousand years old, but it escapes them that the Parisian has been in the making just about that long, and that one does not, therefore, become Parisian by virtue of a Paris address. This little band of bohemians, as grimly singleminded as any evangelical sect, illustrate, by the very ferocity with which they disavow American attitudes, one of the most American of attributes, the inability to believe that time is real. It is this inability which makes them so romantic about the nature of society, and it is this inability which has led them into a total confusion about the nature of experience. Society, it would seem, is a flimsy structure, beneath contempt, designed by and for all the other people, and experience is nothing more than sensation — so many sensations, added up like arithmetic, give one the rich, full life. They thus lose what it was they so bravely set out to find, their own personalities, which, having been deprived of all nourishment, soon cease, in effect, to exist; and they arrive, finally, at a dangerous disrespect for the personalities of others. Though they persist in believing that their present shapelessness is freedom, it is observable that this present freedom is unable to endure either silence or privacy, and demands, for its ultimate expression, a rootless wandering among the cafés. Saint Germain des Près, the heart of the American colony, so far from having absorbed the American student, has been itself transformed, on spring, summer, and fall nights, into a replica, very nearly, of Times Square.

But if this were all one found in the American student colony, one would hardly have the heart to discuss it. If the American found in Europe only confusion, it would obviously be infinitely wiser for him to remain at home. Hidden, however, in the heart of the confusion he encounters here is that which he came so blindly seeking: the terms on which he is related to his country, and to the world. This, which has so grandiose and general a ring, is, in fact, most personal — the American confusion seeming to be based on the very nearly unconscious assumption that it is possible to consider the person apart from all the forces which have produced him. This assumption, however, is itself based on nothing less than our history, which is the history of the total, and willing, alienation of entire peoples from their forebears. What is overwhelmingly clear, it seems, to everyone but ourselves is that this history has created an entirely unprecedented people, with a unique and individual past. It is, indeed, this past which has thrust upon us our present, so troubling role. It is the past lived on the American continent, as against that other past, irrecoverable now on the shores of Europe, which must sustain us in the present. The truth about that past is not that it is too brief, or too superficial, but only that we, having turned our faces so resolutely away from it, have never demanded from it what it has to give. It is this demand which the American student in Paris is forced, at length, to make, for he has otherwise no identity, no reason for being here, nothing to sustain him here. From the vantage point of Europe he discovers his own country. And this is a discovery which not only brings to an end the alienation of the American from himself, but which also makes clear to him, for the first time, the extent of his involvement in the life of Europe.

Equal in Paris

On the 19th of December, in 1949, when I had been living in Paris for a little over a year, I was arrested as a receiver of stolen goods and spent eight days in prison. My arrest came about through an American tourist whom I had met twice in New York, who had been given my name and address and told to look me up. I was then living on the top floor of a ludicrously grim hotel on the rue du Bac, one of those enormous dark, cold, and hideous establishments in which Paris abounds that seem to breathe forth, in their airless, humid, stone-cold halls, the weak light, scurrying chambermaids, and creaking stairs, an odor of gentility long long dead. The place was run by an ancient Frenchman dressed in an elegant black suit which was green with age, who cannot properly be described as bewildered or even as being in a state of shock, since he had really stopped breathing around 1910. There he sat at his desk in the weirdly lit, fantastically furnished lobby, day in and day out, greeting each one of his extremely impoverished and *louche* lodgers with a stately inclination of the head that he had no doubt been taught in some impossibly remote time was the proper way for a *propriétaire* to greet his guests. If it had not been for his daughter, an extremely hardheaded *tricoteuse* — the inclination of *her* head was chilling and abrupt, like the downbeat of an ax — the hotel would certainly have gone

bankrupt long before. It was said that this old man had
not gone farther than the door of his hotel for thirty years,
which was not at all difficult to believe. He looked as
though the daylight would have killed him.

I did not, of course, spend much of my time in this
palace. The moment I began living in French hotels I
understood the necessity of French cafés. This made it
rather difficult to look me up, for as soon as I was out of
bed I hopefully took notebook and fountain pen off to the
upstairs room of the Flore, where I consumed rather a lot
of coffee and, as evening approached, rather a lot of alco-
hol, but did not get much writing done. But one night, in
one of the cafés of St. Germain des Près, I was discovered
by this New Yorker and only because we found ourselves
in Paris we immediately established the illusion that we
had been fast friends back in the good old U.S.A. This
illusion proved itself too thin to support an evening's
drinking, but by that time it was too late. I had committed myself to getting him a room in my hotel the next
day, for he was living in one of the nest of hotels near
the Gare St. Lazare, where, he said, the *propriétaire* was a
thief, his wife a repressed nymphomaniac, the chambermaids "pigs," and the rent a crime. Americans are always
talking this way about the French and so it did not occur
to me that he meant what he said or that he would take
into his own hands the means of avenging himself on the
French Republic. It did not occur to me, either, that the
means which he *did* take could possibly have brought
about such dire results, results which were not less dire
for being also comic-opera.

It came as the last of a series of disasters which had
perhaps been made inevitable by the fact that I had come

to Paris originally with a little over forty dollars in my pockets, nothing in the bank, and no grasp whatever of the French language. It developed, shortly, that I had no grasp of the French character either. I considered the French an ancient, intelligent, and cultured race, which indeed they are. I did not know, however, that ancient glories imply, at least in the middle of the present century, present fatigue and, quite probably, paranoia; that there is a limit to the role of the intelligence in human affairs; and that no people come into possession of a culture without having paid a heavy price for it. This price they cannot, of course, assess, but it is revealed in their personalities and in their institutions. The very word "institutions," from my side of the ocean, where, it seemed to me, we suffered so cruelly from the lack of them, had a pleasant ring, as of safety and order and common sense; one had to come into contact with these institutions in order to understand that they were also outmoded, exasperating, completely impersonal, and very often cruel. Similarly, the personality which had seemed from a distance to be so large and free had to be dealt with before one could see that, if it was large, it was also inflexible and, for the foreigner, full of strange, high, dusty rooms which could not be inhabited. One had, in short, to come into contact with an alien culture in order to understand that a culture was not a community basket-weaving project, nor yet an act of God; was something neither desirable nor undesirable in itself, being inevitable, being nothing more or less than the recorded and visible effects on a body of people of the vicissitudes with which they had been forced to deal. And their great men are revealed as simply another of these vicissitudes, even if, quite against their will, the brief battle of their great men with them has left them richer.

When my American friend left his hotel to move to mine, he took with him, out of pique, a bedsheet belonging to the hotel and put it in his suitcase. When he arrived at my hotel I borrowed the sheet, since my own were filthy and the chambermaid showed no sign of bringing me any clean ones, and put it on my bed. The sheets belonging to *my* hotel I put out in the hall, congratulating myself on having thus forced on the attention of the Grand Hôtel du Bac the unpleasant state of its linen. Thereafter, since, as it turned out, we kept very different hours — I got up at noon, when, as I gathered by meeting him on the stairs one day, he was only just getting in — my new-found friend and I saw very little of each other.

On the evening of the 19th I was sitting thinking melancholy thoughts about Christmas and staring at the walls of my room. I imagine that I had sold something or that someone had sent me a Christmas present, for I remember that I had a little money. In those days in Paris, though I floated, so to speak, on a sea of acquaintances, I knew almost no one. Many people were eliminated from my orbit by virtue of the fact that they had more money than I did, which placed me, in my own eyes, in the humiliating role of a free-loader; and other people were eliminated by virtue of the fact that they enjoyed their poverty, shrilly insisting that this wretched round of hotel rooms, bad food, humiliating concierges, and unpaid bills was the Great Adventure. It couldn't, however, for me, end soon enough, this Great Adventure; there was a real question in my mind as to which would end soonest, the Great Adventure or me. This meant, however, that there were many evenings when I sat in my room, knowing that I couldn't work there, and not knowing what to do, or whom to see. On this particular evening I went down and knocked on the American's door.

There were two Frenchmen standing in the room, who immediately introduced themselves to me as policemen; which did not worry me. I had got used to policemen in Paris bobbing up at the most improbable times and places, asking to see one's *carte d'identité*. These policemen, however, showed very little interest in my papers. They were looking for something else. I could not imagine what this would be and, since I knew I certainly didn't have it, I scarcely followed the conversation they were having with my friend. I gathered that they were looking for some kind of gangster and since I wasn't a gangster and knew that gangsterism was not, insofar as he had one, my friend's style, I was sure that the two policemen would presently bow and say *Merci, messieurs*, and leave. For by this time, I remember very clearly, I was dying to have a drink and go to dinner.

I did not have a drink or go to dinner for many days after this, and when I did my outraged stomach promptly heaved everything up again. For now one of the policemen began to exhibit the most vivid interest in me and asked, very politely, if he might see my room. To which we mounted, making, I remember, the most civilized small talk on the way and even continuing it for some moments after we were in the room in which there was certainly nothing to be seen but the familiar poverty and disorder of that precarious group of people of whatever age, race, country, calling, or intention which Paris recognizes as *les étudiants* and sometimes, more ironically and precisely, as *les nonconformistes.* Then he moved to my bed, and in a terrible flash, not quite an instant before he lifted the bedspread, I understood what he was looking for. We looked at the sheet, on which I read, for the first time, lettered in the most brilliant scarlet I have ever seen, the name of the hotel from which it had been stolen. It was the first time the word *stolen* entered my mind. I had certainly seen the hotel monogram the day I put the sheet on the bed. It had simply meant nothing to me. In New York I had seen hotel monograms on everything from silver to soap and towels. Taking things from New York hotels was practically a custom, though, I suddenly realized, I had never known anyone to take a *sheet.* Sadly, and without a word to me, the inspector took the sheet from the bed, folded it under his arm, and we started back downstairs. I understood that I was under arrest.

And so we passed through the lobby, four of us, two of us very clearly criminal, under the eyes of the old man and his daughter, neither of whom said a word, into the streets where a light rain was falling. And I asked, in French, "But is this very serious?"

For I was thinking, it is, after all, only a sheet, not even new.

"No," said one of them. "It's not serious."

"It's nothing at all," said the other.

I took this to mean that we would receive a reprimand at the police station and be allowed to go to dinner. Later on I concluded that they were not being hypocritical or even trying to comfort us. They meant exactly what they said. It was only that they spoke another language.

In Paris everything is very slow. Also, when dealing with the bureaucracy, the man you are talking to is never the man you have to see. The man you have to see has just gone off to Belgium, or is busy with his family, or has just discovered that he is a cuckold; he will be in next Tuesday at three o'clock, or sometime in the course of the afternoon, or possibly tomorrow, or, possibly, in the next five minutes. But if he is coming in the next five minutes he will be far too busy to be able to see you today. So that I suppose I was not really astonished to learn at the commissariat that nothing could possibly be done about us before The Man arrived in the morning. But no, we could not go off and have dinner and come back in the morning. Of course he knew that we *would* come back — that was not the question. Indeed, there was no question: we would simply have to stay there for the night. We were placed in a cell which rather resembled a chicken coop. It was now about seven in the evening and I relinquished the thought of dinner and began to think of lunch.

I discouraged the chatter of my New York friend and this left me alone with my thoughts. I was beginning to be frightened and I bent all my energies, therefore, to keeping my panic under control. I began to realize that I was in a country I knew nothing about, in the hands of a people I did not understand at all. In a similar situation in New York I would have had some idea of what to do because I would have had some idea of what to expect. I am not speaking now of legality which, like most of the poor, I had never for an instant trusted, but of the temperament of the people with whom I had to deal. I had become very accomplished in New York at guessing and, therefore, to a limited extent manipulating to my advantage the reactions of the white world. But this was not

New York. None of my old weapons could serve me here. I did not know what they saw when they looked at me. I knew very well what Americans saw when they looked at me and this allowed me to play endless and sinister variations on the role which they had assigned me; since I knew that it was, for them, of the utmost importance that they never be confronted with what, in their own personalities, made this role so necessary and gratifying to them, I knew that they could never call my hand or, indeed, afford to know what I was doing; so that I moved into every crucial situation with the deadly and rather desperate advantages of bitterly accumulated perception, of pride and contempt. This is an awful sword and shield to carry through the world, and the discovery that, in the game I was playing, I did myself a violence of which the world, at its most ferocious, would scarcely have been capable, was what had driven me out of New York. It was a strange feeling, in this situation, after a year in Paris, to discover that my weapons would never again serve me as they had.

It was quite clear to me that the Frenchmen in whose hands I found myself were no better or worse than their American counterparts. Certainly their uniforms frightened me quite as much, and their impersonality, and the threat, always very keenly felt by the poor, of violence, was as present in that commissariat as it had ever been for me in any police station. And I had seen, for example, what Paris policemen could do to Arab peanut vendors. The only difference here was that I did not understand these people, did not know what techniques their cruelty took, did not know enough about their personalities to see danger coming, to ward it off, did not know on what ground to meet it. That evening in the commissariat I was not a despised black man. They would simply have laughed at me if I had behaved like one. For them, I was an American. And here it was they who had the advantage, for that word, *Américain*, gave them some idea, far from inaccurate, of what to expect from me. In order to corroborate none of their ironical expectations I said nothing and did nothing — which was not the way any Frenchman, white or black, would have reacted. The question thrusting up from the bottom of my mind was not *what* I was, but *who*. And this question, since a *what* can get by with skill but a *who* demands resources, was my first real intimation of what humility must mean.

In the morning it was still raining. Between nine and ten o'clock a black Citroën took us off to the Ile de la Cité, to the great, gray Préfecture. I realize now that the questions I put to the various policemen who escorted us were always answered in such a way as to corroborate what I wished to hear. This was not out of politeness, but simply out of indifference — or, possibly, an ironical pity — since each of the policemen knew very well that nothing would speed or halt the machine in which I had become entangled. They knew I did not know this and there was certainly no point in their telling me. In one way or another I would certainly come out at the other side — for they also knew that being found with a stolen bedsheet in one's possession was not a crime punishable by the guillotine. (They had the advantage over me there, too, for there were certainly moments later on when I was not so sure.) If I did *not* come out at the other side — well, that was just too bad. So, to my question, put while we were in the Citroën — "Will it be over today?" — I re-

ceived a *"Oui, bien sûr."* He was not lying. As it turned
out, the *procès-verbal* was over that day. Trying to be
realistic, I dismissed, in the Citroën, all thoughts of lunch
and pushed my mind ahead to dinner.

At the Préfecture we were first placed in a tiny cell, in
which it was almost impossible either to sit or to lie down.
After a couple of hours of this we were taken down to an
office, where, for the first time, I encountered the owner
of the bedsheet and where the *procès-verbal* took place.
This was simply an interrogation, quite chillingly clipped
and efficient (so that there was, shortly, no doubt in one's
own mind that one *should* be treated as a criminal), which
was recorded by a secretary. When it was over, this report
was given to us to sign. One had, of course, no choice but
to sign it, even though my mastery of written French was
very far from certain. We were being held, according to
the law in France, incommunicado, and all my angry
demands to be allowed to speak to my embassy or to see
a lawyer met with a stony *"Oui, oui. Plus tard."* The
procès-verbal over, we were taken back to the cell, before
which, shortly, passed the owner of the bedsheet. He said
he hoped we had slept well, gave a vindictive wink, and
disappeared.

By this time there was only one thing clear: that we had
no way of controlling the sequence of events and could
not possibly guess what this sequence would be. It seemed
to me, since what I regarded as the high point — the
procès-verbal — had been passed and since the hotel-
keeper was once again in possession of his sheet, that we
might reasonably expect to be released from police custody in a matter of hours. We had been detained now
for what would soon be twenty-four hours, during which

time I had learned only that the official charge against me was *receleur*. My mental shifting, between lunch and dinner, to say nothing of the physical lack of either of these delights, was beginning to make me dizzy. The steady chatter of my friend from New York, who was determined to keep my spirits up, made me feel murderous; I was praying that some power would release us from this freezing pile of stone before the impulse became the act. And I was beginning to wonder what was happening in that beautiful city, Paris, which lived outside these walls. I wondered how long it would take before anyone casually asked, "But where's Jimmy? He hasn't been around" — and realized, knowing the people I knew, that it would take several days.

Quite late in the afternoon we were taken from our cells; handcuffed, each to a separate officer; led through a maze of steps and corridors to the top of the building; fingerprinted; photographed. As in movies I had seen, I was placed against a wall, facing an old-fashioned camera, behind which stood one of the most completely cruel and indifferent faces I had ever seen, while someone next to me and, therefore, just outside my line of vision, read off in a voice from which all human feeling, even feeling of the most base description, had long since fled, what must be called my public characteristics — which, at that time and in that place, seemed anything but that. He might have been roaring to the hostile world secrets which I could barely, in the privacy of midnight, utter to myself. But he was only reading off my height, my features, my approximate weight, my color — that color which, in the United States, had often, odd as it may sound, been my salvation — the color of my hair, my age, my nationality.

A light then flashed, the photographer and I staring at each other as though there was murder in our hearts, and then it was over. Handcuffed again, I was led downstairs to the bottom of the building, into a great enclosed shed in which had been gathered the very scrapings off the Paris streets. Old, old men, so ruined and old that life in them seemed really to prove the miracle of the quickening power of the Holy Ghost — for clearly their life was no longer their affair, it was no longer even their burden, they were simply the clay which had once been touched. And men not so old, with faces the color of lead and the consistency of oatmeal, eyes that made me think of stale *café-au-lait* spiked with arsenic, bodies which could take in food and water — any food and water — and pass it out, but which could not do anything more, except possibly, at midnight, along the riverbank where rats scurried, rape. And young men, harder and crueler than the Paris stones, older by far than I, their chronological senior by some five to seven years. And North Africans, old and young, who seemed the only living people in this place because they yet retained the grace to be bewildered. But they were not bewildered by being in this shed: they were simply bewildered because they were no longer in North Africa. There was a great hole in the center of this shed, which was the common toilet. Near it, though it was impossible to get very far from it, stood an old man with white hair, eating a piece of camembert. It was at this point, probably, that thought, for me, stopped, that physiology, if one may say so, took over. I found myself incapable of saying a word, not because I was afraid I would cry but because I was afraid I would vomit. And I did not think any longer of the city of Paris but my

mind flew back to that home from which I had fled. I was
sure that I would never see it any more. And it must have
seemed to me that my flight from home was the cruelest
trick I had ever played on myself, since it had led me here,
down to a lower point than any I could ever in my life
have imagined — lower, far, than anything I had seen
in that Harlem which I had so hated and so loved, the
escape from which had soon become the greatest direction
of my life. After we had been here an hour or so a func-
tionary came and opened the door and called out our
names. And I was sure that *this* was my release. But I
was handcuffed again and led out of the Préfecture into
the streets — it was dark now, it was still raining — and
before the steps of the Préfecture stood the great police
wagon, doors facing me, wide open. The handcuffs were
taken off, I entered the wagon, which was peculiarly
constructed. It was divided by a narrow aisle, and on
each side of the aisle was a series of narrow doors. These
doors opened on a narrow cubicle, beyond which was a
door which opened onto another narrow cubicle: three or
four cubicles, each private, with a locking door. I was
placed in one of them; I remember there was a small vent
just above my head which let in a little light. The door
of my cubicle was locked from the outside. I had no idea
where this wagon was taking me and, as it began to move,
I began to cry. I suppose I cried all the way to prison,
the prison called Fresnes, which is twelve kilometers outside of Paris.

For reasons I have no way at all of understanding,
prisoners whose last initial is A, B, or C are always sent
to Fresnes; everybody else is sent to a prison called, rather
cynically it seems to me, La Santé. I will, obviously, never

be allowed to enter La Santé, but I was told by people who certainly seemed to know that it was infinitely more unbearable than Fresnes. This arouses in me, until today, a positive storm of curiosity concerning what I promptly began to think of as The Other Prison. My colleague in crime, occurring lower in the alphabet, had been sent there and I confess that the minute he was gone I missed him. I missed him because he was not French and because he was the only person in the world who knew that the story I told was true.

For, once locked in, divested of shoelaces, belt, watch, money, papers, nailfile, in a freezing cell in which both the window and the toilet were broken, with six other adventurers, the story I told of *l'affaire du drap de lit* elicited only the wildest amusement or the most suspicious disbelief. Among the people who shared my cell the first three days no one, it is true, had been arrested for anything much more serious — or, at least, not serious in my eyes. I remember that there was a boy who had stolen a knitted sweater from a *monoprix*, who would probably, it was agreed, receive a six-month sentence. There was an older man there who had been arrested for some kind of petty larceny. There were two North Africans, vivid, brutish, and beautiful, who alternated between gaiety and fury, not at the fact of their arrest but at the state of the cell. None poured as much emotional energy into the fact of their arrest as I did; they took it, as I would have liked to take it, as simply another unlucky happening in a very dirty world. For, though I had grown accustomed to thinking of myself as looking upon the world with a hard, penetrating eye, the truth was that they were far more realistic about the world than I, and more nearly right about it. The gap between us, which only a gesture I made could have bridged, grew steadily, during thirty-six hours, wider. I could not make any gesture simply because they frightened me. I was unable to accept my imprisonment as a fact, even as a temporary fact. I could not, even for a moment, accept my present companions as *my* companions. And they, of course, felt this and put it down, with perfect justice, to the fact that I was an American.

There was nothing to do all day long. It appeared that we would one day come to trial but no one knew when. We were awakened at seven-thirty by a rapping on what I believe is called the Judas, that small opening in the door of the cell which allows the guards to survey the prisoners. At this rapping we rose from the floor — we slept on straw pallets and each of us was covered with one thin blanket — and moved to the door of the cell. We peered through the opening into the center of the prison, which was, as I remember, three tiers high, all gray stone and gunmetal steel, precisely that prison I had seen in movies, except that, in the movies, I had not known that it was cold in prison. I had not known that when one's shoelaces and belt have been removed one is, in the strangest way, demoralized. The necessity of shuffling and the necessity of holding up one's trousers with one hand turn one into a rag doll. And the movies fail, of course, to give one any idea of what prison food is like. Along the corridor, at seven-thirty, came three men, each pushing before him a great garbage can, mounted on wheels. In the garbage can of the first was the bread — this was passed to one through the small opening in the door. In the can of the second was the coffee. In the can of the third was what was always called *la soupe*, a pallid paste of potatoes which had certainly been bubbling on the back of the prison stove long before that first, so momentous revolution. Naturally, it was cold by this time and, starving as I was, I could not eat it. I drank the coffee — which was not coffee — because it was hot, and spent the rest of the day, huddled in my blanket, munching on the bread. It was not the French bread one bought in bakeries. In the evening the same procession returned. At ten-thirty the lights went out. I had a recurring dream, each night, a nightmare which always involved my mother's fried chicken. At the moment I was about to eat it came the rapping at the door. Silence is really all I remember of those first three days, silence and the color gray.

I am not sure now whether it was on the third or the fourth day that I was taken to trial for the first time. The days had nothing, obviously, to distinguish them from one another. I remember that I was very much aware that Christmas Day was approaching and I wondered if I was really going to spend Christmas Day in prison. And I remember that the first trial came the day before Christmas Eve.

On the morning of the first trial I was awakened by hearing my name called. I was told, hanging in a kind of void between my mother's fried chicken and the cold prison floor, *"Vous préparez. Vous êtes extrait"* — which simply terrified me, since I did not know what interpretation to put on the word *"extrait,"* and since my cellmates had been amusing themselves with me by telling terrible stories about the inefficiency of French prisons, an inefficiency so extreme that it had often happened that someone who was supposed to be taken out and tried found himself on the wrong line and was guillotined instead. The best way of putting my reaction to this is to say that, though I knew they were teasing me, it was simply not possible for me to totally *dis*believe them. As far as I was concerned, once in the hands of the law in France, anything could happen. I shuffled along with the others who were *extrait* to the center of the prison, trying, rather, to linger in the office, which seemed the only warm spot in the whole world, and found myself again in that dreadful wagon, and was carried again to the Ile de la Cité, this time to the Palais de Justice. The entire day, except for ten minutes, was spent in one of the cells, first waiting to be tried, then waiting to be taken back to prison.

For I was *not* tried that day. By and by I was handcuffed and led through the halls, upstairs to the courtroom where I found my New York friend. We were placed together, both stage-whisperingly certain that this was the end of our ordeal. Nevertheless, while I waited for our case to be called, my eyes searched the courtroom, looking for a face I knew, hoping, anyway, that there was someone there who knew *me*, who would carry to someone outside the news that I was in trouble. But there was no one I knew there and I had had time to realize that there was probably only one man in Paris who could help me, an American patent attorney for whom I had worked as an office boy. He could have helped me because he had a quite solid position and some prestige and would have testified that, while working for him, I had handled large sums of money regularly, which made it rather unlikely that I would stoop to trafficking in bedsheets. However, he was somewhere in Paris, probably at this very moment enjoying a snack and a glass of wine and as

far as the possibility of reaching him was concerned, he
might as well have been on Mars. I tried to watch the proceedings and to make my mind a blank. But the proceedings were not reassuring. The boy, for example, who had
stolen the sweater *did* receive a six-month sentence. It
seemed to me that all the sentences meted out that day
were excessive; though, again, it seemed that all the people
who were sentenced that day had made, or clearly were
going to make, crime their career. This seemed to be the
opinion of the judge, who scarcely looked at the prisoners
or listened to them; it seemed to be the opinion of the
prisoners, who scarcely bothered to speak in their own
behalf; it seemed to be the opinion of the lawyers, state
lawyers for the most part, who were defending them. The
great impulse of the courtroom seemed to be to put these
people where they could not be seen — and not because
they were offended at the crimes, unless, indeed, they
were offended that the crimes were so petty, but because
they did not wish to know that their society could be
counted on to produce, probably in greater and greater
numbers, a whole body of people for whom crime was the
only possible career. Any society inevitably produces its
criminals, but a society at once rigid and unstable can do
nothing whatever to alleviate the poverty of its lowest
members, cannot present to the hypothetical young man
at the crucial moment that so-well-advertised right path.
And the fact, perhaps, that the French are the earth's least
sentimental people and must also be numbered among the
most proud aggravates the plight of their lowest, youngest,
and unluckiest members, for it means that the idea of
rehabilitation is scarcely real to them. I confess that this
attitude on their part raises in me sentiments of exaspera-

tion, admiration, and despair, revealing as it does, in both the best and the worst sense, their renowned and spectacular hard-headedness.

Finally our case was called and we rose. We gave our names. At the point that it developed that we were American the proceedings ceased, a hurried consultation took place between the judge and what I took to be several lawyers. Someone called out for an interpreter. The arresting officer had forgotten to mention our nationalities and there was, therefore, no interpreter in the court. Even if our French had been better than it was we would not have been allowed to stand trial without an interpreter. Before I clearly understood what was happening, I was handcuffed again and led out of the courtroom. The trial had been set back for the 27th of December.

I have sometimes wondered if I would *ever* have got out of prison if it had not been for the older man who had been arrested for the mysterious petty larceny. He was acquitted that day and when he returned to the cell — for he could not be released until morning — he found me sitting numbly on the floor, having just been prevented, by the sight of a man, all blood, being carried back to *his* cell on a stretcher, from seizing the bars and screaming until they let me out. The sight of the man on the stretcher proved, however, that screaming would not do much for me. The petty-larceny man went around asking if he could do anything in the world outside for those he was leaving behind. When he came to me I, at first, responded, "No, nothing" — for I suppose I had by now retreated into the attitude, the earliest I remember, that of my father, which was simply (since I had lost his God) that nothing could help me. And I suppose I will remember with gratitude until I die the fact that the man now insisted: *"Mais, êtes-vous sûr?"* Then it swept over me that he was going *outside* and he instantly became my first contact since the Lord alone knew how long with the outside world. At the same time, I remember, I did not really believe that he would help me. There was no reason why he should. But I gave him the phone number of my attorney friend and my own name.

So, in the middle of the next day, Christmas Eve, I shuffled downstairs again, to meet my visitor. He looked extremely well fed and sane and clean. He told me I had nothing to worry about any more. Only not even he could do anything to make the mill of justice grind any faster. He would, however, send me a lawyer of his acquaintance who would defend me on the 27th, and he would himself, along with several other people, appear as a character witness. He gave me a package of Lucky Strikes (which the turnkey took from me on the way upstairs) and said that, though it was doubtful that there would be any celebration in the prison, he would see to it that I got a fine Christmas dinner when I got out. And this, somehow, seemed very funny. I remember being astonished at the discovery that I was actually laughing. I was, too, I imagine, also rather disappointed that my hair had not turned white, that my face was clearly not going to bear any marks of tragedy, disappointed at bottom, no doubt, to realize, facing him in that room, that far worse things had happened to most people and that, indeed, to paraphrase my mother, if this was the worst thing that ever happened to me I could consider myself among the luckiest people ever to be born. He injected — my visitor — into my solitary nightmare common sense, the world, and the hint of blacker things to come.

The next day, Christmas, unable to endure my cell, and feeling that, after all, the day demanded a gesture, I asked to be allowed to go to Mass, hoping to hear some music. But I found myself, for a freezing hour and a half, locked in exactly the same kind of cubicle as in the wagon which had first brought me to prison, peering through a slot placed at the level of the eye at an old Frenchman, hatted, overcoated, muffled, and gloved, preaching in this language which I did not understand, to this row of wooden boxes, the story of Jesus Christ's love for men.

The next day, the 26th, I spent learning a peculiar kind of game, played with match-sticks, with my cellmates. For, since I no longer felt that I would stay in this cell forever, I was beginning to be able to make peace with it for a time. On the 27th I went again to trial and, as had been predicted, the case against us was dismissed. The story of the *drap de lit,* finally told, caused great merriment in the courtroom, whereupon my friend decided that the French were "great." I was chilled by their merriment, even though it was meant to warm me. It could only remind me of the laughter I had often heard at home, laughter which I had sometimes deliberately elicited. This laughter is the laughter of those who consider themselves to be at a safe remove from all the wretched, for whom the pain of the living is not real. I had heard it so often in my native land that I had resolved to find a place where I would never hear it any more. In some deep, black, stony, and liberating way, my life, in my own eyes, began during that first year in Paris, when it was borne in on me that this laughter is universal and never can be stilled.

Stranger in the Village

From all available evidence no black man had ever set foot in this tiny Swiss village before I came. I was told before arriving that I would probably be a "sight" for the village; I took this to mean that people of my complexion were rarely seen in Switzerland, and also that city people are always something of a "sight" outside of the city. It did not occur to me — possibly because I am an American — that there could be people anywhere who had never seen a Negro.

It is a fact that cannot be explained on the basis of the inaccessibility of the village. The village is very high, but it is only four hours from Milan and three hours from Lausanne. It is true that it is virtually unknown. Few people making plans for a holiday would elect to come here. On the other hand, the villagers are able, presumably, to come and go as they please — which they do: to another town at the foot of the mountain, with a population of approximately five thousand, the nearest place to see a movie or go to the bank. In the village there is no movie house, no bank, no library, no theater; very few radios, one jeep, one station wagon; and, at the moment, one typewriter, mine, an invention which the woman next door to me here had never seen. There are about six hundred people living here, all Catholic — I conclude this from the fact that the Catholic church is open all year round, whereas the Protestant chapel, set off on a hill a little removed from the village, is open only in the summertime when the tourists arrive. There are four or five hotels, all closed now, and four or five *bistros,* of which, however, only two do any business during the winter. These two do not do a great deal, for life in the village seems to end around nine or ten o'clock. There are a few stores, butcher, baker, *épicerie,* a hardware store, and a money-changer — who cannot change travelers' checks, but must send them down to the bank, an operation which takes two or three days. There is something called the *Ballet Haus,* closed in the winter and used for God knows what, certainly not ballet, during the summer. There seems to be only one schoolhouse in the village, and this for the quite young children; I suppose this to mean that their older brothers and sisters at some point descend from these mountains in order to complete their education — possibly, again, to the town just below. The landscape is absolutely forbidding, mountains towering on all four sides, ice and snow as far as the eye can reach. In this white wilderness, men and women and children move all day, carrying washing, wood, buckets of milk or water, sometimes skiing on Sunday afternoons. All week long boys and young men are to be seen shoveling snow off the rooftops, or dragging wood down from the forest in sleds.

The village's only real attraction, which explains the tourist season, is the hot spring water. A disquietingly high proportion of these tourists are cripples, or semi-cripples, who come year after year — from other parts of Switzerland, usually — to take the waters. This lends the village, at the height of the season, a rather terrifying air of sanctity, as though it were a lesser Lourdes. There

is often something beautiful, there is always something
awful, in the spectacle of a person who has lost one of his
faculties, a faculty he never questioned until it was gone,
and who struggles to recover it. Yet people remain people,
on crutches or indeed on deathbeds; and wherever I
passed, the first summer I was here, among the native
villagers or among the lame, a wind passed with me — of
astonishment, curiosity, amusement, and outrage. That
first summer I stayed two weeks and never intended to
return. But I did return in the winter, to work; the village
offers, obviously, no distractions whatever and has the
further advantage of being extremely cheap. Now it is
winter again, a year later, and I am here again. Everyone
in the village knows my name, though they scarcely ever
use it, knows that I come from America — though, this,
apparently, they will never really believe: black men come
from Africa — and everyone knows that I am the friend
of the son of a woman who was born here, and that I am
staying in their chalet. But I remain as much a stranger
today as I was the first day I arrived, and the children
shout *Neger! Neger!* as I walk along the streets.

It must be admitted that in the beginning I was far too
shocked to have any real reaction. In so far as I reacted
at all, I reacted by trying to be pleasant — it being a great
part of the American Negro's education (long before he
goes to school) that he must make people "like" him. This
smile-and-the-world-smiles-with-you routine worked about
as well in this situation as it had in the situation for which
it was designed, which is to say that it did not work at all.
No one, after all, can be liked whose human weight and
complexity cannot be, or has not been, admitted. My
smile was simply another unheard-of phenomenon which

allowed them to see my teeth — they did not, really, see my smile and I began to think that, should I take to snarling, no one would notice any difference. All of the physical characteristics of the Negro which had caused me, in America, a very different and almost forgotten pain were nothing less than miraculous — or infernal — in the eyes of the village people. Some thought my hair was the color of tar, that it had the texture of wire, or the texture of cotton. It was jocularly suggested that I might let it all grow long and make myself a winter coat. If I sat in the sun for more than five minutes some daring creature was certain to come along and gingerly put his fingers on my hair, as though he were afraid of an electric shock, or put his hand on my hand, astonished that the color did not rub off. In all of this, in which it must be conceded there was the charm of genuine wonder and in which there was certainly no element of intentional unkindness, there was yet no suggestion that I was human: I was simply a living wonder.

I knew that they did not mean to be unkind, and I know it now; it is necessary, nevertheless, for me to repeat this to myself each time that I walk out of the chalet. The children who shout *Neger!* have no way of knowing the echoes this sound raises in me. They are brimming with good humor and the more daring swell with pride when I stop to speak with them. Just the same, there are days when I cannot pause and smile, when I have no heart to play with them; when, indeed, I mutter sourly to myself, exactly as I muttered on the streets of a city these children have never seen, when I was no bigger than these children are now: *Your* mother *was a nigger.* Joyce is right about history being a nightmare — but it may be the nightmare from which no one *can* awaken. People are trapped in history and history is trapped in them.

There is a custom in the village — I am told it is repeated in many villages — of "buying" African natives for the purpose of converting them to Christianity. There stands in the church all year round a small box with a slot for money, decorated with a black figurine, and into this box the villagers drop their francs. During the *carnaval* which precedes Lent, two village children have their faces blackened — out of which bloodless darkness their blue eyes shine like ice — and fantastic horsehair wigs are placed on their blond heads; thus disguised, they solicit among the villagers for money for the missionaries in Africa. Between the box in the church and the blackened children, the village "bought" last year six or eight African natives. This was reported to me with pride by the wife of one of the *bistro* owners and I was careful to express astonishment and pleasure at the solicitude shown by the village for the souls of black folk. The *bistro* owner's wife beamed with a pleasure far more genuine than my own and seemed to feel that I might now breathe more easily concerning the souls of at least six of my kinsmen.

I tried not to think of these so lately baptized kinsmen, of the price paid for them, or the peculiar price they themselves would pay, and said nothing about my father, who having taken his own conversion too literally never, at bottom, forgave the white world (which he described as heathen) for having saddled him with a Christ in whom, to judge at least from their treatment of him, they themselves no longer believed. I thought of white men arriving for the first time in an African village, strangers there, as I am a stranger here, and tried to imagine the astounded populace touching their hair and marveling at the color of their skin. But there is a great difference between being the first white man to be seen by Africans and being the first black man to be seen by whites. The white man takes the astonishment as tribute, for he arrives to conquer and to convert the natives, whose inferiority in relation to himself is not even to be questioned; whereas I, without a thought of conquest, find myself among a people whose culture controls me, has even, in a sense, created me, people who have cost me more in anguish and rage than they will ever know, who yet do not even know of my existence. The astonishment with which I might have greeted them, should they have stumbled into my African village a few hundred years ago, might have rejoiced their hearts. But the astonishment with which they greet me today can only poison mine.

And this is so despite everything I may do to feel differently, despite my friendly conversations with the *bistro* owner's wife, despite their three-year-old son who has at last become my friend, despite the *saluts* and *bonsoirs* which I exchange with people as I walk, despite the fact that I know that no individual can be taken to task for what history is doing, or has done. I say that the culture of these people controls me — but they can scarcely be held responsible for European culture. America comes out of Europe, but these people have never seen America, nor have most of them seen more of Europe than the hamlet at the foot of their mountain. Yet they move with an authority which I shall never have; and they regard me, quite rightly, not only as a stranger in their village but as a suspect latecomer, bearing no credentials, to everything they have — however unconsciously — inherited.

For this village, even were it incomparably more remote and incredibly more primitive, is the West, the West
onto which I have been so strangely grafted. These people
cannot be, from the point of view of power, strangers anywhere in the world; they have made the modern world, in
effect, even if they do not know it. The most illiterate
among them is related, in a way that I am not, to Dante,
Shakespeare, Michelangelo, Aeschylus, Da Vinci, Rembrandt, and Racine; the cathedral at Chartres says something to them which it cannot say to me, as indeed would
New York's Empire State Building, should anyone here
ever see it. Out of their hymns and dances come Bee-
thoven and Bach. Go back a few centuries and they are
in their full glory — but I am in Africa, watching the
conquerors arrive.

The rage of the disesteemed is personally fruitless, but
it is also absolutely inevitable; this rage, so generally dis-
counted, so little understood even among the people whose
daily bread it is, is one of the things that makes history.
Rage can only with difficulty, and never entirely, be
brought under the domination of the intelligence and is
therefore not susceptible to any arguments whatever.
This is a fact which ordinary representatives of the *Herrenvolk*, having never felt this rage and being unable to
imagine it, quite fail to understand. Also, rage cannot be
hidden, it can only be dissembled. This dissembling de-
ludes the thoughtless, and strengthens rage and adds, to
rage, contempt. There are, no doubt, as many ways of
coping with the resulting complex of tensions as there are
black men in the world, but no black man can hope ever to
be entirely liberated from this internal warfare — rage,
dissembling, and contempt having inevitably accompanied

his first realization of the power of white men. What is crucial here is that, since white men represent in the black man's world so heavy a weight, white men have for black men a reality which is far from being reciprocal; and hence all black men have toward all white men an attitude which is designed, really, either to rob the white man of the jewel of his naïveté, or else to make it cost him dear.

The black man insists, by whatever means he finds at his disposal, that the white man cease to regard him as an exotic rarity and recognize him as a human being. This is a very charged and difficult moment, for there is a great deal of will power involved in the white man's naïveté. Most people are not naturally reflective any more than they are naturally malicious, and the white man prefers to keep the black man at a certain human remove because it is easier for him thus to preserve his simplicity and avoid being called to account for crimes committed by his forefathers, or his neighbors. He is inescapably aware, nevertheless, that he is in a better position in the world than black men are, nor can he quite put to death the suspicion that he is hated by black men therefore. He does not wish to be hated, neither does he wish to change places, and at this point in his uneasiness he can scarcely avoid having recourse to those legends which white men have created about black men, the most usual effect of which is that the white man finds himself enmeshed, so to speak, in his own language which describes hell, as well as the attributes which lead one to hell, as being as black as night.

Every legend, moreover, contains its residuum of truth, and the root function of language is to control the universe by describing it. It is of quite considerable significance that black men remain, in the imagination, and in overwhelming numbers in fact, beyond the disciplines of salvation; and this despite the fact that the West has been "buying" African natives for centuries. There is, I should hazard, an instantaneous necessity to be divorced from this so visibly unsaved stranger, in whose heart, moreover, one cannot guess what dreams of vengeance are being nourished; and, at the same time, there are few things on earth more attractive than the idea of the unspeakable liberty which is allowed the unredeemed. When, beneath the black mask, a human being begins to make himself felt one cannot escape a certain awful wonder as to what kind of human being it is. What one's imagination makes of other people is dictated, of course, by the laws of one's own personality and it is one of the ironies of black-white relations that, by means of what the white man imagines the black man to be, the black man is enabled to know who the white man is.

I have said, for example, that I am as much a stranger in this village today as I was the first summer I arrived, but this is not quite true. The villagers wonder less about the texture of my hair than they did then, and wonder rather more about me. And the fact that their wonder now exists on another level is reflected in their attitudes and in their eyes. There are the children who make those delightful, hilarious, sometimes astonishingly grave overtures of friendship in the unpredictable fashion of children; other children, having been taught that the devil is a black man, scream in genuine anguish as I approach. Some of the older women never pass without a friendly greeting, never pass, indeed, if it seems that they will be able to engage me in conversation; other women look down or look away or rather contemptuously smirk. Some of the men drink with me and suggest that I learn how to ski — partly, I gather, because they cannot imagine what I would look like on skis — and want to know if I am married, and ask questions about my *métier*. But some of the men have accused *le sale nègre* — behind my back — of stealing wood and there is already in the eyes of some of them that peculiar, intent, paranoiac malevolence which one sometimes surprises in the eyes of American white men when, out walking with their Sunday girl, they see a Negro male approach.

There is a dreadful abyss between the streets of this village and the streets of the city in which I was born, between the children who shout *Neger!* today and those who shouted *Nigger!* yesterday — the abyss is experience, the American experience. The syllable hurled behind me today expresses, above all, wonder: I am a stranger here. But I am not a stranger in America and the same syllable riding on the American air expresses the war my presence has occasioned in the American soul.

For this village brings home to me this fact: that there was a day, and not really a very distant day, when Americans were scarcely Americans at all but discontented Europeans, facing a great unconquered continent and strolling, say, into a marketplace and seeing black men for the first time. The shock this spectacle afforded is suggested, surely, by the promptness with which they decided that these black men were not really men but cattle. It is true that the necessity on the part of the settlers of the New World of reconciling their moral assumptions with the fact — and the necessity — of slavery enhanced immensely the charm of this idea, and it is also true that this idea expresses, with a truly American bluntness, the attitude which to varying extents all masters have had toward all slaves.

But between all former slaves and slave-owners and the drama which begins for Americans over three hundred years ago at Jamestown, there are at least two differences to be observed. The American Negro slave could not suppose, for one thing, as slaves in past epochs had supposed and often done, that he would ever be able to wrest the power from his master's hands. This was a supposition which the modern era, which was to bring about such vast changes in the aims and dimensions of power, put to death; it only begins, in unprecedented fashion, and with dreadful implications, to be resurrected today. But even had this supposition persisted with undiminished force, the American Negro slave could not have used it to lend his condition dignity, for the reason that this supposition rests on another: that the slave in exile yet remains related to his past, has some means — if only in memory — of revering and sustaining the forms of his former life, is able, in short, to maintain his identity.

This was not the case with the American Negro slave. He is unique among the black men of the world in that his past was taken from him, almost literally, at one blow. One wonders what on earth the first slave found to say to the first dark child he bore. I am told that there are Haitians able to trace their ancestry back to African kings, but any American Negro wishing to go back so far will find his journey through time abruptly arrested by the signature on the bill of sale which served as the entrance paper for his ancestor. At the time — to say nothing of the circumstances — of the enslavement of the captive black man who was to become the American Negro, tl ere was not the remotest possibility that he would ever take power from his master's hands. There was no reason to suppose that his situation would ever change, nor was there, shortly, anything to indicate that his situation had ever been different. It was his necessity, in the words of E. Franklin Frazier, to find a "motive for living under American culture or die." The identity of the American Negro comes out of this extreme situation, and the evolution of this identity was a source of the most intolerable anxiety in the minds and the lives of his masters.

For the history of the American Negro is unique also in this: that the question of his humanity, and of his rights therefore as a human being, became a burning one for several generations of Americans, so burning a question that it ultimately became one of those used to divide the nation. It is out of this argument that the venom of the epithet *Nigger!* is derived. It is an argument which Europe has never had, and hence Europe quite sincerely fails to understand how or why the argument arose in the first place, why its effects are so frequently disastrous and always so unpredictable, why it refuses until today to be entirely settled. Europe's black possessions remained — and do remain — in Europe's colonies, at which remove they represented no threat whatever to European identity. If they posed any problem at all for the European conscience, it was a problem which remained comfortingly abstract: in effect, the black man, *as a man,* did not exist for Europe. But in America, even as a slave, he was an inescapable part of the general social fabric and no American could escape having an attitude toward him. Americans attempt until today to make an abstraction of the Negro, but the very nature of these abstractions reveals the tremendous effects the presence of the Negro has had on the American character.

When one considers the history of the Negro in America it is of the greatest importance to recognize that the moral beliefs of a person, or a people, are never really as tenuous as life — which is not moral — very often causes them to appear; these create for them a frame of reference and a necessary hope, the hope being that when life has done its worst they will be enabled to rise above themselves and to triumph over life. Life would scarcely be bearable if this hope did not exist. Again, even when the worst has been said, to betray a belief is not by any means to have put oneself beyond its power; the betrayal of a belief is not the same thing as ceasing to believe. If this were not so there would be no moral standards in the world at all. Yet one must also recognize that morality is based on ideas and that all ideas are dangerous — dangerous because ideas can only lead to action and where the action leads no man can say. And dangerous in this respect: that confronted with the impossibility of remaining faithful to one's beliefs, and the equal impossibility of becoming free of them, one can be driven to the most inhuman excesses. The ideas on which American beliefs are based are not, though Americans often seem to think so, ideas which originated in America. They came out of Europe. And the establishment of democracy on the American continent was scarcely as radical a break with the past as was the necessity, which Americans faced, of broadening this concept to include black men.

This was, literally, a hard necessity. It was impossible, for one thing, for Americans to abandon their beliefs, not only because these beliefs alone seemed able to justify the sacrifices they had endured and the blood that they had spilled, but also because these beliefs afforded them their only bulwark against a moral chaos as absolute as the physical chaos of the continent it was their destiny to conquer. But in the situation in which Americans found themselves, these beliefs threatened an idea which, whether or not one likes to think so, is the very warp and woof of the heritage of the West, the idea of white supremacy.

Americans have made themselves notorious by the shrillness and the brutality with which they have insisted on this idea, but they did not invent it; and it has escaped the world's notice that those very excesses of which Americans have been guilty imply a certain, unprecedented uneasiness over the idea's life and power, if not, indeed, the idea's validity. The idea of white supremacy rests simply on the fact that white men are the creators of civilization (the present civilization, which is the only one that matters; all previous civilizations are simply "contributions" to our own) and are therefore civilization's guardians and defenders. Thus it was impossible for Americans to accept the black man as one of themselves, for to do so was to jeopardize their status as white men. But not so to accept him was to deny his human reality, his human weight and complexity, and the strain of denying the overwhelmingly undeniable forced Americans into rationalizations so fantastic that they approached the pathological.

At the root of the American Negro problem is the necessity of the American white man to find a way of living with the Negro in order to be able to live with himself. And the history of this problem can be reduced to the means used by Americans — lynch law and law, segregation and legal acceptance, terrorization and concession — either to come to terms with this necessity, or to find a way around it, or (most usually) to find a way of doing both these things at once. The resulting spectacle, at once foolish and dreadful, led someone to make the quite accurate observation that "the Negro-in-America is a form of insanity which overtakes white men."

In this long battle, a battle by no means finished, the unforeseeable effects of which will be felt by many future generations, the white man's motive was the protection of his identity; the black man was motivated by the need to establish an identity. And despite the terrorization which the Negro in America endured and endures sporadically until today, despite the cruel and totally inescapable ambivalence of his status in his country, the battle for his identity has long ago been won. He is not a visitor to the West, but a citizen there, an American; as American as the Americans who despise him, the Americans who fear him, the Americans who love him — the Americans who became less than themselves, or rose to be greater than themselves by virtue of the fact that the challenge he represented was inescapable. He is perhaps the only black man in the world whose relationship to white men is more terrible, more subtle, and more meaningful than the relationship of bitter possessed to uncertain possessor. His survival depended, and his development depends, on his ability to turn his peculiar status in the Western world to his own advantage and, it may be, to the very great advantage of that world. It remains for him to fashion out of his experience that which will give him sustenance, and a voice.

The cathedral at Chartres, I have said, says something to the people of this village which it cannot say to me; but it is important to understand that this cathedral says something to me which it cannot say to them. Perhaps they are struck by the power of the spires, the glory of the windows; but they have known God, after all, longer than I have known him, and in a different way, and I am terrified by the slippery bottomless well to be found in the crypt, down which heretics were hurled to death, and by the obscene, inescapable gargoyles jutting out of the stone and seeming to say that God and the devil can never be divorced. I doubt that the villagers think of the devil when they face a cathedral because they have never been identified with the devil. But I must accept the status which myth, if nothing else, gives me in the West before I can hope to change the myth.

Yet, if the American Negro has arrived at his identity by virtue of the absoluteness of his estrangement from his past, American white men still nourish the illusion that there is some means of recovering the European innocence, of returning to a state in which black men do not exist. This is one of the greatest errors Americans can make. The identity they fought so hard to protect has, by virtue of that battle, undergone a change: Americans are as unlike any other white people in the world as it is possible to be. I do not think, for example, that it is too much to suggest that the American vision of the world — which allows so little reality, generally speaking, for any of the darker forces in human life, which tends until today to paint moral issues in glaring black and white — owes a great deal to the battle waged by Americans to maintain between themselves and black men a human separation which could not be bridged. It is only now beginning to be borne in on us — very faintly, it must be admitted, very slowly, and very much against our will — that this vision of the world is dangerously inaccurate, and perfectly useless. For it protects our moral high-mindedness at the terrible expense of weakening our grasp of reality. People who shut their eyes to reality simply invite their own destruction, and anyone who insists on remaining in a state of innocence long after that innocence is dead turns himself into a monster.

The time has come to realize that the interracial drama acted out on the American continent has not only created a new black man, it has created a new white man, too. No road whatever will lead Americans back to the simplicity of this European village where white men still have the luxury of looking on me as a stranger. I am not, really, a stranger any longer for any American alive. One of the things that distinguishes Americans from other people is that no other people has ever been so deeply involved in the lives of black men, and vice versa. This fact faced, with all its implications, it can be seen that the history of the American Negro problem is not merely shameful, it is also something of an achievement. For even when the worst has been said, it must also be added that the perpetual challenge posed by this problem was always, somehow, perpetually met. It is precisely this black-white experience which may prove of indispensable value to us in the world we face today. This world is white no longer, and it will never be white again.

DATE			